MAKER**SPACES**

Other Redleaf Press Books by Michelle Kay Compton
and Robin Chappele Thompson

*StoryMaking: The Maker Movement Approach to
Literacy for Early Learners*

Makerspaces

Remaking Your Play and STEAM Early Learning Areas

Robin Chappele Thompson, PhD • Michelle Kay Compton, MA

Redleaf Press®
www.redleafpress.org
800-423-8309

Published by Redleaf Press
10 Yorkton Court
St. Paul, MN 55117
www.redleafpress.org

First edition 2020
Cover design and photograph by Michelle Lee Lagerroos
Interior design by Erin Kirk New
Typeset in Sentinel
Printed in the United States of America
27 26 25 24 23 22 21 20   1 2 3 4 5 6 7 8

Library of Congress Cataloging-in-Publication Data

Names: Thompson, Robin, 1960- author. | Compton, Michelle Kay, author.
Title: Makerspaces : remaking your play and STEAM early learning areas /
  Robin Chappele Thompson, Michelle Kay Compton.
Description: First edition. | St. Paul, MN : Redleaf Press, 2020. |
  Includes bibliographical references and index. | Summary: "Makerspaces
  focuses on how to cultivate the maker mind-set in the youngest learners,
  focusing on how to engage young children in maker-centered learning,
  design, and introduce makerspaces, or select and use tools and materials
  that are open-ended during making for our youngest children"— Provided
  by publisher.
Identifiers: LCCN 2020004889 (print) | LCCN 2020004890 (ebook) | ISBN
  9781605547138 (paperback) | ISBN 9781605547145 (ebook)
Subjects: LCSH: Maker movement in education. | Makerspaces. | Early
  childhood education—Activity programs.
Classification: LCC LB1029.M35 T56 2020 (print) | LCC LB1029.M35
(ebook)
  | DDC 372.21—dc23
LC record available at https://lccn.loc.gov/2020004889
LC ebook record available at https://lccn.loc.gov/2020004890

Printed on acid-free paper

For each of LaLa's future makers.

—RCT

For my two little makers who invite me into their
world of playing and making each day.

—MKC

Contents

Acknowledgments

Michelle, we are a true testament to the Maker Cycle as together we imagine the possibilities, play with our ideas and dreams, and make it all a reality as we get to share our makerspaces. I'm thankful that your boys are willing participants, for they bring joy to my days with their imaginations and adventures. I am thankful for your brilliant mind and most especially that you keep me laughing through it all. As you know, you are loved by my entire family, and we consider you and yours as part of the family.

Angela Knapek and Shannon Rivard, thank you for always being willing to be willing. I have fallen in love with your students and their brilliant minds. Thank you for inviting me into your classrooms to imagine, play, make, and share with you and your children. I am thankful for teachers like you who will try something new and innovative, tinker with it, try some more, and make something beautiful for your children. I appreciate you more than you know.

Chris O'Hara, thank you for welcoming me at the Manatee County Downtown Central Library for our pop-up makerspaces. I've met some wonderful families and children at the library, and I look forward to more playing and making in the future.

Soar in 4 (https://soarin4.org), a community initiative for early learners that supports the Suncoast Campaign for Grade-Level Reading and invites our families and children to imagine, play, make, and share, has been a wonderful partner in inspiring StoryMaking and makerspaces along our journey. A big thank-you to Mary Glass and the board members of the Manatee Education Foundation for the constant support of Soar in 4 and the many opportunities for thinking outside the box. Working with children and families through the Manatee Education Foundation, the School District of Manatee County, the ArtCenter Manatee, the Bishop Museum of Science and Nature, the Manatee County Central Library, and the Early Learning Coalition of Manatee County has been my great joy, and I am thankful that I get to work in a community whose priorities include families and our youngest learners. Together we are building a stronger community filled with families who know that their children learn through play.

Materials to inspire you from each of our categories (wood, nature, plastic, glass, metal, textiles, and paper)

A Book for All Makers

I am a maker and a thinker.
I imagine, play, hack, and tinker.
Empty spaces and stuff are all I need
to showcase my ideas for the world to see.

Making, or the maker movement, has recently made its way to both formal and informal learning environments. We initially engaged our young learners in the maker movement through StoryMaking, using its practices as the framework for learning. We found that our young makers use the Maker Cycle to imagine, play, make, and share not only stories but also ideas, projects, opinions, and thinking. Through our research and observations (in classrooms, centers, museums, libraries, and homeschool communities), we have discovered that all young children can identify as makers, given the resources and spaces for making.

Makers, Makerspaces, and Materials

As we learned more about the maker movement, its learning practices, and the development of a maker mindset, our teachers wanted to create makerspaces in their classrooms. We define a *makerspace* as any place where children of all ages use materials and tools to imagine, play, make, and share their ideas, projects, stories, or thinking. Any place can be a makerspace. A *maker* is anyone who uses materials to make something important or interesting to them. In our makerspaces children are the makers: artists, collagists, builders, sculptors, performers, inventors, weavers, storytellers, and writers who interact with open-ended materials. Given opportunities to explore a variety of materials in makerspaces, they take on the identity of makers.

Making can seem intimidating to educators because much of the information on it addresses older children, targets technology, and seems to focus on coding, robotics, and other topics that might require special expertise. We learned that our colleagues at museums, schools, libraries, universities, and child care centers wanted to design inviting makerspaces but either didn't know where to begin or didn't know how to sustain the makerspaces they set up. This book will ensure that

What Is a Maker?

Creative mind to imagine what you can make with materials.

Practicing with tools to hack and repurpose materials.

Eyes to observe art and imagine new ideas.

A kind heart to make something for yourself or others.

Curious ears for listening to the ideas of others.

Sharing mouth to make a plan and share what you made with others.

Tinkering hands for playing and making with materials.

Exploring feet to find the resources you need to make.

"What Is a Maker?" Anchor chart

the maker movement is accessible to all those who work with young children, ages two to eight, in informal (libraries, museums) and formal (classrooms, home care providers) settings, at universities with early childhood and elementary education departments, and at home in families. We provide a foundation for the design and setup of inviting makerspaces and suggest developmentally appropriate inspirations, materials, and tools. We also provide lots of photos of different makerspaces in a variety of settings, step-by-step suggestions, and ideas for sustaining interest and learning in each of the makerspaces, as well as lesson plans for use as you develop your own makerspaces.

We have experimented with making and makerspaces in schools, libraries, museums, and other learning spaces. We've tinkered with ideas, tried them out, iterated, reflected, and tried again. We've worked with toddlers, preschool children, and early elementary students. We understand that if you work in a formal educational setting, there may be expectations for achieving proficiency in accordance with standards. This book provides ideas for converting typical areas and spaces found in educational settings, both informal and formal, into sustainable makerspaces that use open-ended materials—materials that do not have a right or wrong expectation for use—so young children can enact the learning practices of the maker movement.

Why Are Makerspaces Important?

The maker movement in education includes "creating the physical, mental, and social conditions for a child to learn through real-life experiences that are personal and meaningful" (Dougherty 2016, x). The *physical* conditions are the learning spaces, which can serve as the third teacher. Makerspaces offer inspiration and support for new learning while also ensuring access to materials and resources that scaffold this learning (Biermeier 2015; Ceppi and Zini 1998; Compton and Thompson 2018; Malaguzzi 1998; Peppler, Halverson, and Kafai 2016). The *mental* conditions are goals that support academic proficiency on developmental milestones and standards, as well as the embodiment of a maker mindset. It has been suggested that makerspaces are communities of practice that provide multiple pathways for learning, opportunities for developing fluency and competence for the learning goals, and open-ended materials that encourage self-expression, promote creativity, and support the development of agency and character (Blikstein and Worsley 2016; Brahms and Crowley 2016; Clapp et al. 2017; Peppler, Halverson, and Kafai 2016; Wardrip and Brahms 2015). The *social* conditions include the collaborative learning culture found in makerspaces, where materials and resources are shared, children have opportunities to contribute to one another's work, and both processes and products are shared and celebrated (Brahms and Wardrip 2016; Resnick, Eidman-Aadahl, and Dougherty 2016; Wardrip and Brahms 2014).

Developing a Maker Mindset

A mindset is "a way of seeing and being in the world" (Clapp et al. 2017, 87). Researchers have defined characteristics of a maker mindset, or positive qualities we hope to cultivate in children (Barell 2013; Dougherty 2016; Regalla 2016). We combined this research with what we observed in classrooms, libraries, museums, and centers and developed the following list of indicators for use as you work toward the development of a maker mindset in your young children:

- Makers exhibit a sense of wonder. Our young children "exhibit curiosity when they play with new materials, explore new spaces, and investigate their worlds" (Compton and Thompson 2018, 53). Children are naturally curious about their worlds, and as we design our makerspaces we want to consider the materials and spaces that "give children the opportunity for wonder, mystery, and discovery; an environment that speaks to young children's inherent curiosity and innate yearning for exploration" (Heard and McDonough 2009, 8).

- Makers are mindful observers. As children become keen observers, they notice details in their worlds. They learn to focus their attention and spend time thinking about their surroundings. Learning to look closely can be practiced in many ways. "Students might draw, make lists, or name the parts of a particular object; they might verbally describe intricacies. . . . These practices also cultivate a habit of slowing down" (Clapp et al. 2017, 131–32). Our goal is to develop mindful observers who become deep thinkers.

- Makers are STREAM innovators. Our young children make discoveries about themselves and their worlds as they innovate with materials, spaces, and processes. They discover new uses for common materials, invent representations for unfamiliar materials, and develop ideas for processes as they play and make. They cross-pollinate among learning spaces and materials, creating opportunities for interdisciplinary learning. Introducing STREAM (science, technology, reading/literacy, engineering, arts, and math) topics and focus lessons gives them the tools to think across disciplines, one of the essential qualities of a successful innovator (Wagner 2012).

- Makers develop social-emotional efficacy. Social-emotional competence is built when children work and play together. They need opportunities to learn and practice sharing, taking turns, and self-regulating. Bailey (2015) encourages educators to notice helpful and kind acts, both publicly and one-on-one with children. As children practice these acts, they are internalizing social-emotional efficacy.

- Makers enact a growth mindset. "A growth mindset promotes the belief that capabilities can be continuously developed, improved, and refined through experiences that involve success, mistakes, and persistence" (Regalla 2016, 267). Children have opportunities to build and enact a growth mindset as they imagine, play, make, and share. They build an "I can" attitude as they make choices, select materials, and create things that are meaningful to them. They persevere and figure out the hard parts, gain self-efficacy, and build character. Finally, they get to reflect and share with an inclusive community, discussing their mistakes, asking for help when they need it, and celebrating their successes.

- Makers share and collaborate. When children have the opportunity to share what they are making in a maker talk, they can draw on their community to ask for advice and celebrate their processes and products. The maker movement uplifts others' efforts and promotes a culture of sharing ideas so each person can innovate and accomplish their imagined goals. Regalla states, "Through exchanging ideas, helping one another succeed, and celebrating both successes and challenges, a culture of collaboration and sharing is cultivated" (2016, 267).

The Maker Cycle

Our Maker Cycle is where the inquiry process starts for teaching and learning, as the children engage with materials, one another, and their imaginations. During the cycle children encounter authentic problems ("How can I make this fit?" or "I can't make this work. How do I do it?"). Our conception of the maker movement includes igniting children's imaginations and following their interests; engaging them with interesting and open-ended materials through playing and making; and celebrating each child's ideas, stories, projects, and histories by sharing with one another and their communities (classroom, families, local community). This teaching and learning process is represented by our Maker Cycle.

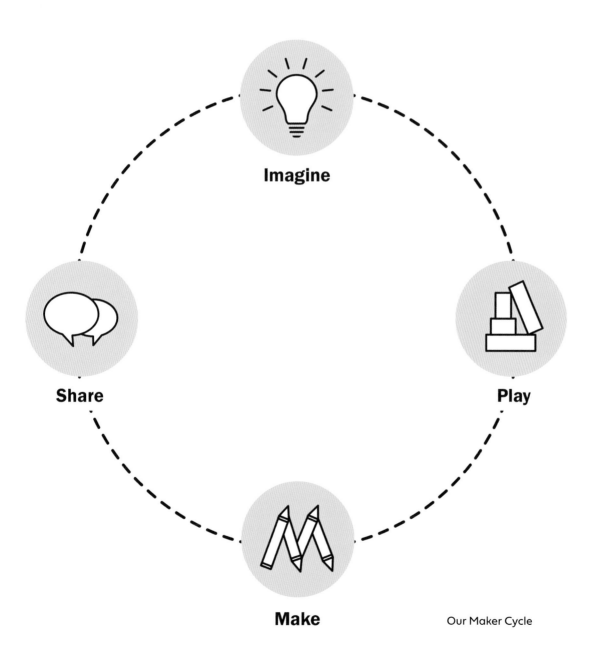

Imagine

Play

Make

Share

Our Maker Cycle

- Imagine: We provide children with provocations and invitations that inspire them to wonder and inquire. We use unusual and interesting materials, common materials experienced in new ways, children's literature, a focus lesson, or anything else that inspires young children.
- Play: It has been shown again and again that young children learn through play. During play they interact with materials and one another, become familiar with the forms and functions of materials, and start to develop social-emotional efficacy (Christakis 2017; Edwards, Gandini, and Forman 1998; Gopnik 2010; Heard and McDonough 2009; Mraz, Porcelli, and Tyler 2016; NAEYC 2009; Resnick 2016; Wohlwend 2008).
- Make: After playing for a sufficient amount of time, children begin to create and build what they've imagined. During this time they develop agency, build character, and enact the learning practices of the maker movement (Brahms and Crowley 2016; Clapp et al. 2017; Resnick 2016; Wardrip and Brahms 2014).
- Share: Often children are excited to share what they've made or how they've made it, whether it is an idea, project, or story. They share in languages other than oral (painting, dance, sculpture) to demonstrate their learning and celebrate their successes with one another during maker talks.

Learning Practices of the Maker Mindset

Researchers have described the learning practices embodied during participation in making within a framework (Brahms and Crowley 2016; Compton and Thompson 2018; Wardrip and Brahms 2015). These learning practices are the behaviors enacted by children in our Maker Cycle that indicate they are learning. Children may exhibit them in the order presented or skip around, depending on the context of their imagining, playing, making, and sharing. In the Maker Cycle, children enact the following learning practices of the maker movement:

- inquire
- tinker
- seek and share resources
- hack and repurpose
- express intent
- develop fluency
- simplify to complexify

Each learning practice encapsulates aspects of what it takes to develop a maker mindset, our overarching goal. It's impossible to enact the learning practices without growing a maker mindset, as they are inextricably linked. Below we identify the learning practices of the maker movement and highlight associated elements of simultaneously developing a maker mindset.

INQUIRE

Young children naturally have a sense of curiosity and wonder about their worlds. Their openness and willingness to explore and question leads to deep learning and discovery. When children are awed by their everyday worlds, you will hear, "What is that?" or "How can I make it do that?" Development of a sense of wonder is one of the characteristics of a maker mindset, and creating opportunities for children to explore, ask questions, and be inspired aids that process.

TINKER

When children play around with materials and tools, figuring out their forms and functions, they are tinkering. Karen Wilkinson and Mike Petrich define *tinkering* as "thinking with your hands and learning through doing" (2014, 13). Children may try several iterations of one idea or representation before they are satisfied with the outcome. In the process they are often evaluating the properties of the materials and tools. You will know children are tinkering when you notice them manipulating and interacting with materials, trying to figure out their affordances, saying, "This won't bend" or "I'm trying to make a castle with blocks, but it keeps falling." Self-awareness and self-management come to the fore when things don't work as planned. Development of social-emotional efficacy through play is characteristic of a maker mindset.

SEEK AND SHARE RESOURCES

Learning spaces for young children offer an abundance of resources and materials. The children may use each other as resources during playing and making, asking, "Where did you get that idea?" or "How did you make that?" This indicates recognition of their not-knowing and shows a desire to learn. Materials can also serve as resources for children by inspiring questions and discovery and accommodating manipulations as the children figure out materials' affordances and limits. Books offer good information as children try to solve problems, study, figure things out, and get inspired. Anchor charts showing techniques for using materials and tools provide the information and reminders children need to move forward in their thinking. As children share their materials, tools, and expertise, they develop social-emotional efficacy by building relationship skills, making responsible decisions, and developing a disposition to share and collaborate. Development of social-emotional efficacy and a disposition to share and collaborate are components of a maker mindset.

HACK AND REPURPOSE

Children use materials and tools in innovative ways. They often assign new uses and representations to a familiar material, disassociating it from its original purpose. A craft stick can be a fort wall, a character's body, or a tool to stir paint. Children can easily repurpose open-ended materials, which do not have a specific purpose or intent. Reusing and recycling materials during playing and making can lead to conversations about conserving resources and sharing what we have. This builds a disposition to share and collaborate and encourages a growth mindset, building confidence and an "I can do it" attitude, all part of a maker mindset.

EXPRESS INTENT

Some children express intent shortly after they are inspired by a story or material. It might sound like, "I want to make a robot today!" or "I want to go to the construction makerspace." Other children do not make a short- or long-term plan until after they've investigated materials and had some time to play and explore. Children's identities are developed through playing, making, and sharing, and with that comes a sense of agency and a growth mindset. You might hear, "I can do this!" or "I did it all by myself!" Offering choice helps children make decisions about where they want to play and make and provides opportunities for them to develop agency and character. A growth mindset is a characteristic of a maker mindset.

DEVELOP FLUENCY

As children practice playing and making with materials and tools, they develop fluency with their uses. They develop self-efficacy and begin to take risks and innovate. As children become proficient with materials and tools, they become resources for other children and move forward in their own thinking for deeper and more complex learning. Becoming fluent with the uses of materials and tools takes practice, effort, and persistence and contributes to building a growth mindset, one of the characteristics of the maker mindset.

SIMPLIFY TO COMPLEXIFY

As children become familiar with the tools and materials found in different makerspaces, you might see them borrowing materials from one makerspace and combining them with tools and materials from another to make their idea or project. Combining simple materials from various spaces and contexts creates new meanings and complex representations. For example, we had watercolor in the arts makerspace and wood and fabric materials for puppets in the performance makerspace. Cornelia decided to paint her wooden puppet's body with the watercolors and created a unique character who was "feeling blue." This interdisciplinary approach or STREAM innovation is part of creating a maker mindset. As children explore materials, they become mindful observers, studying the parts, purposes, and complexities in order to represent their unique ideas, stories, and projects (Clapp et al. 2017). While every maker's process is different, the stages of the Maker Cycle typically align with the learning practices and the development of a maker mindset as shown in the following chart.

Learning Practices and Development of a Maker Mindset through the Maker Cycle

Maker Cycle	Imagine	Play and Make						Share
Learning Practices of the Maker Movement	Inquire	Tinker	Seek Resources	Hack and Repurpose	Express Intent	Develop Fluency	Simplify to Complexify	Share
Maker Mindset	Sense of Wonder	Mindful Observation Social-Emotional Efficacy Enactment of a Growth Mindset STREAM Innovation						Share and Collaborate

Activity versus Investigation

When planning your makerspaces, we advocate for a focus on the powerful learning practices of the maker instead of creating activities for a specific science or mathematical standard, as Chalufour and Worth (2004) illustrate in their Young Scientist series. There are some key differences between an activity-based thematic study and an in-depth investigation. When an educator notices an interest among the children (such as cars) or a specific topic in standards or curricular programs (such as three-dimensional shapes), they might select materials and a particular type of block for an activity. Toy cars and boats and unit blocks might accompany a question such as "How can you build a bridge for these cars to cross over the river?" The children will engage in this activity, of course, but the teacher did all the imagining and thinking for this space. The toys selected to accompany the building activity—the materials—were not open-ended. The car represents a car and the boat a boat. The task will help children make connections to math and science topics, but it has little to do with the exploration of scientific and engineering concepts within the Maker Cycle.

An open-ended approach to makerspaces allows children to be creative thinkers. The educator can observe what information the children learn and communicate as they make. To create an investigation rather than an activity, incorporate loose parts, a subcategory of open-ended materials that we define as any open-ended, recyclable, or found item that can be transported, manipulated, innovated, and used for exploration and multiple representations in a variety of contexts (Daly and Beloglovsky 2015). Stimulate thinking by presenting loose parts to symbolize the vehicles and asking open-ended questions, such as "What structures can you make with these materials?" An in-depth investigation of bridges in the building makerspace allows children to communicate what they know and express interest in other topics as well. When you allow children to express their intentions for making with open-ended materials, you are not only engaging them in an inquiry process (the Maker Cycle) but also developing the maker mindset. Research supports the use of open-ended materials in growing a maker mindset, as any open-ended material can inspire stories, ideas, and projects. And all areas can be remade into makerspaces that build the maker mindset (Daly and Beloglovsky 2015; Gauntlett and Thomsen 2013; Heard and McDonough 2009; McGalliard 2016).

The Important Role of Materials in Our Makerspaces

Research suggests that materials can inspire children to learn as they go through our Maker Cycle and enact the learning practices of the maker movement (inquire, tinker, seek and share resources, hack and repurpose, express intent, develop fluency, and simplify to complexify) as they develop a maker mindset. The maker movement is grounded in Seymour Papert's constructionism: "the building of artifacts, be it a program, robot, or sand castle, that can be shared with others" (Peppler, Halverson, and Kafai 2016, 5).

Not only can materials inspire children as they make, but we observed that interactions with materials often resulted in the enactment of the learning practices. Research supports the integral role of materials in learning as children think through making and engage with materials (Dolphijn and van der Tuin 2012; Ingold 2012; Kind 2014; Penfold 2019; Taguchi 2011). Evidence of learning from these encounters with materials and one another can be found in the learning practices of the maker movement. Learning is not necessarily the result of one encounter; rather, multiple encounters form a network of connections and interactions between children and materials. Materials lend themselves to different types of learning, depending on what the child brings to the encounter (history, background knowledge, interest) and the attributes of the material (form, function). Humans and materials dialogue with one another throughout an encounter: for example, "Hey. Why won't you bend? I'm trying to bend you. I will break you in two instead." The materials do not actually speak, of course, but they present forces and flows in interaction with children, who become active participants as they learn from and are transformed by materials. Connections, interactions, and transformations with materials lead children to new understandings about themselves, one another, and the world, understandings reflected in the assemblages children imagine, make, and share. The development of a maker mindset through the enactment of the learning practices of the maker movement depends on materials and their contribution to the learning and development of our children (Dolphijn and van der Tuin 2012; Ingold 2012; Penfold 2019; Taguchi 2011). The selection and exploration of materials are so important to our makerspaces that we have begun each chapter with a story documenting children's first encounter and interactions with the materials in the featured makerspace.

STEAM Learning in the Makerspace

Many books and programs drawing on the maker movement have adopted STEM (science, technology, engineering, and math) or STEAM (science, technology, engineering, arts, and math) learning as part of the learning activities they suggest. When we refer to technology, it's important to realize that the first step toward proficiency is developing a fluency with concrete tools and understanding how they work prior to playing and making in the digital world. We added the *R* to represent reading and literacy. We can't leave that out! Literacy is an important component to our children's learning.

Makerspaces are a natural setting for STEAM learning; therefore, we highlight in each chapter some specific, research-based connections to the STEAM disciplines in the featured makerspace (NGSS Lead States 2013; NSTA 2014; Texley and Ruud 2018). This section also shows that you do not need a separate STEAM area outside of your makerspaces. Our goal is to help you integrate learning across the domains within your makerspaces and show how you can present an interdisciplinary approach to learning in your makerspaces.

What to Expect

If you are new to the maker movement and have not yet experimented with setting up makerspaces, this book offers a chronological plan for transforming existing classroom areas into makerspaces for children from toddlers to eight years old. If you are an experienced makerspace creator already, are planning a makerspace on a particular topic, or want to set up a pop-up makerspace—a temporary makerspace in an informal learning environment—feel free to skip to the relevant chapter. Detailed lists and photos will aid you in replicating a makerspace for your purposes. Imitation is the first stage of learning, right? However, we challenge you to internalize the components of our makerspaces in order to invent your own. These are the components that form part of each chapter's structure:

1. Inspiration and support: ideas, images, charts, focus lessons, children's literature, and techniques
2. Main material: the first material used, often a foundation or canvas
3. Loose parts: open-ended materials introduced to complexify the main material
4. Tools and attachments: items used to modify, manipulate, and connect materials

A thorough understanding of these components will help you become the innovators and designers of your makerspaces.

Chapter 1 provides an overview of the design and setup of new makerspaces, including supplies that you probably have in your classroom already, and presents a template for the remaining chapters. Each chapter begins with notes on a child interacting with materials from that makerspace, a discussion of the makerspace's purpose and place in the chronological progression, and its STREAM connections. We then identify relevant materials and tools along a continuum from low-tech arts and crafts to high-tech explorations such as coding and robots. These continuums will help you plan materials and next steps for your makerspaces. We then invite you to "Imagine Making" your makerspace, giving examples of inspiration, materials, loose parts, and tools that have worked well in our makerspaces and providing photos of different "Spaces for Playing and Making." We offer examples of how to document learning in makerspaces, share a sample focus lesson and some books to inspire makers, and recommend next steps for growing your makerspace.

Chapter 2 starts with the art area and shows how to use inspiration, main materials, and tools to transform it into an arts makerspace. It combines process- and product-based approaches to focus on the elements of art while also considering aesthetics and beauty. Chapter 3 builds on the arts makerspace and suggests a new makerspace, collage. Collage is a three-dimensional fine art in which materials or loose parts are assembled on a surface. Collage is an inexpensive, inspiring, and easy makerspace to set up, and we think you'll love it. Chapter 4 explains how to transform your block area into a construction makerspace, offering numerous suggestions for materials, from different types of blocks and cardboard to woodworking, Lego bricks, and codeable moving blocks. Chapter 5 shows how to turn your playdough area into a sculpture makerspace, including suggestions for making three-dimensional sculptures with playdough, clay, foil, wire, and products, such as Squishy Circuits. Chapter 6 adds movement, dialogue, and action to the previous makerspaces and turns your housekeeping or dramatic play area into a performance makerspace, complete with costume design, set design, props, and character development. Chapter 7 transforms your sensory area into magical small worlds where makers become inventors of new landscapes, inhabitants, and worlds. Chapter 8 looms on the horizon with threading, lacing, weaving, and sewing, transforming your lacing boards and activities into a fiber arts makerspace celebrating children's efforts as they play and make with these unfamiliar materials. Since our Maker Cycle emphasizes the importance of sharing with peers, family, or other like-minded makers, chapter 9 expands on maker talks as a means of encouraging discourse developing a supportive maker community. We also highlight an idea for a maker talk in the "Share" section of the focus lesson at the end of each chapter.

Next Steps in Transforming Spaces

We've thrown a lot at you in this introduction, but do not be afraid. Please stick with us! You can transform your play areas into makerspaces using what you already have in your space. You do not need to spend a bunch of money, become a technology guru, or get rid of all your current stuff. With a few simple tweaks, you can create beautiful and productive makerspaces for your children. And this transformation does not have to happen all at once. We recommend doing a little bit at a time. Choose a favorite space and add one new idea to ignite children's imaginations, or remake a tired space that the children no longer frequent. We'll show you some simple changes that will invite children back into that space. Do it in a way that makes you comfortable. We have lots of inspiration for you, but it's up to you to decide which ideas you want to use, how you want to use them, and when you want to try them out. We just ask that you keep us posted and show us how you hack and repurpose our ideas to build your own makerspaces!

You are the maker, the designer, the tinkerer of your own spaces. The examples, photos, descriptions, and tips you will find in these pages are intended to inspire you in creating makerspaces that will meet the needs of the children you serve. As you plan and teach, you, too, are participating in our Maker Cycle and engaging in the learning practices of the maker movement. We invite you to join our maker community and share your discoveries and makerspaces on our website (www .storymakers.us) and with your colleagues. Let's begin our journey together, right here, right now, and imagine powerful makerspaces where children can have a better education, rooted in play, and opportunities to grow as artists, collagists, builders, sculptors, performers, inventors, storytellers, and writers . . . makers.

Materials brought from home that inspired children as they imagined, played, made, and shared

CHAPTER 1

Designing and Setting Up Your Makerspaces

As I explore materials in front of me,
My imagination awakes with possibility.
As a maker, I discover new ways to create.
My materials guide and help me communicate.

Stories to Inspire Making

They looked like plain white paper bags. Nothing special. Some were a bit crumpled, for their adventures had been rough on them. But to the children, they were so much more than plain white bags. They were bags full of secrets—treasure bags, bursting at the seams. The children, imagining magical riches within, couldn't wait to investigate.

An invitation for children to imagine, play, and make with found materials

Paper bags brought from home, filled with found materials, recyclables, and loose parts

Materials inspire wonder and awe.

Finally, it was time to peek into the bags and discover the jewels, precious metals, and other materials. What wonders did these treasure troves hold?

Everyday objects became magical to children as they scavenged through the loot: shiny parade beads of every color and sticks and broken necklaces with sparkling jewels and shells and screws of all sizes. Discussions of pirates and mermaids and underwater adventures began immediately. Then everyone gathered around as another bag was emptied into the large, transparent plastic bin. There were shoelaces and pipe cleaners and string and bottle caps and cardboard and paper clips and

As more children brought in materials, we moved them to a larger bin.

Children exploring, tinkering, hacking, and repurposing materials brought from home

twine and rocks and straws. Each child was invited to fill a container and take it to their table to play, explore, sort, organize, stack, dump, and make.

Each child placed their treasures on a metallic cookie sheet that further reflected their precious bits and pieces. They played and cut and touched and sorted and traded and arranged and talked about their favorites. They made swing sets at the park, built trucks, went on pretend journeys with their materials, and shared their adventures with their friends. They were awed by the materials and their worlds. The materials had conveyed to them that they were going to make wonderful discoveries together.

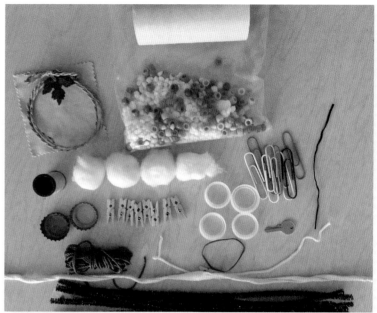

Each picture captures the contents of one of the treasure bags.

This was the beginning of a wonderful adventure with materials. The children imagined, played, made, and shared the stories, ideas, projects, and thinking that were inspired by the materials they had gathered, collected, brought from home, explored, questioned, investigated, and organized. At the close of the adventure, the materials found homes in containers in each of the makerspaces.

We introduce each chapter with children's interactions with materials because we have found that the "desire to construct meaning with visual materials is often inspired by the materials themselves. Beautiful, interesting, and appealing materials call out to be touched, used, and played with" (Massey 2017, 7). This introduction, focused on how materials lead to discovery and learning, launches the makerspace highlighted in the chapter. This first story featured excitement about the materials our students and families gathered and brought to the classroom at the beginning of the year.

Why Create Multiple Makerspaces?

Just as you probably have multiple centers, STEM challenge areas, or play spaces in your current learning space, we suggest that you design and set up multiple makerspaces in your current spaces with materials you already have on hand. Not to worry: we will provide inspirations along the way.

You will transform one space at a time, using what you already have. By transforming your current areas into makerspaces, you are simply adding intention and purpose to your play areas. Using the space you already have, the inspirations—ideas, examples, lessons, questions, children's book recommendations—in this book, and simple materials that you probably already have, you will spark children's curiosity, invite them to notice and pay attention to their environments, inspire them to think across domains, encourage social-emotional learning, and celebrate as they share and collaborate, building a maker mindset.

Remaking Classroom Spaces into Makerspaces

In this section we offer examples of how you can transform your existing spaces into the makerspace featured in each chapter. Follow these steps to get started:

- Select an area to transform. Do you want to transform an area that your children do not use often? A space that your children love? A new space?
- How many children do you anticipate playing and making in that space? This will determine what materials and space you will need.
- Inspiration and Support: Select a children's book and create a question that matches your purpose for the makerspace.
- Main Materials: Take an inventory of the main materials you have on hand and select one or two to place in the space at first. Consider removing, storing, or reorganizing items that can be introduced as a new main material later in the year to sustain play and interest.
- Loose Parts: Consider the loose parts you have and choose one to three to incorporate into the children's playing and making at first.
- Tools and Attachments: Select tools, if any, that will support making with the main materials and loose parts.

Organization/ Aesthetics

We organize our main materials and loose parts by composition. Our categories include plastic, textiles, metal, nature, wood, glass, and paper. If this helps you, try it. If not, use a system that works for you.

Ideally your initial makerspace setup will interest the children for several weeks. Over time, or if you see children's interest waning, add a new or different main material or select a new category of loose parts to replace the current offering. New loose parts spark wonder and curiosity for making. There is no right or wrong. Use whatever you have that aligns with your current unit of study or theme and will instill a sense of wonder in your children.

Arts and Crafts

← — →

High Tech

Consider whether your materials are closed-ended (have an intended right or wrong use) or open-ended (can represent many things; no prescribed use). The goal is to slowly introduce more open-ended materials and eventually put aside closed-ended materials that do not hold children's interest until you have more open-ended than closed-ended materials in your transformed areas.

Notice that children are in the makerspaces for longer periods of time and remain more engaged with the open-ended materials.

Notice and document the enactment of the learning practices as the children play and make.

Consider introducing more complex tools and attachments as the children gain fluency with the main materials and loose parts.

If you notice the children getting bored, rotate in some new and interesting materials or have a focus lesson on a new technique.

Analyze the learning practices children have enacted and notice their growth toward a maker mindset.

Introduce more complex materials, such as take-aparts, digital apps, and high-tech options as available.

STREAM Learning in Makerspaces

Elements of STREAM learning can be found throughout each makerspace, and we provide targeted language stems for use with your students as they go deeper with their learning. We also highlight opportunities for interdisciplinary learning and innovation in each makerspace. We begin here with some overarching goals aligned with each of the STREAM domains.

Prompts to Ensure STREAM Learning Connections

	Makers will do the following:
Science	• Explore the world around them ("What can you imagine making with these materials?")
Technology	• Select and use appropriate tools with fluency ("What tools can you use as you play and make with these materials?")
Reading/Literacy	• Grow their identities as readers and authors and communicate with others ("How would you like to share your project, idea, thinking, or story?") • Find meaning in read-alouds and recognize story structure ("What stories can you imagine with these materials?")
Engineering	• Encounter problems and figure out possible solutions ("What techniques can you use to figure out how to work with these materials?")
Arts	• Identify and apply the elements of art in a developmentally appropriate way ("How have you used your knowledge of color/shape/line/space/design as you make?") • Grow their maker and artist identities ("What can you imagine making with these materials as an artist/painter/collagist/sculptor?")
Mathematics	• Recognize shapes, count, measure, and compare ("What [tools, measurements, shapes, amounts] can you use to make what you imagined?")

Imagine Making a New Makerspace

Imagine is the first step of the Maker Cycle for teachers and young children alike. The "Imagine Making a Makerspace" section of each chapter highlights goals or purposes for the makerspace; resources for inspiration and support in the design and setup; and the main materials, loose parts, tools, and attachments that might be used in each makerspace. We present photos to document a makerspace that we designed and then discuss some of the many possible adaptations and variations.

In accordance with the premise of backward design, we begin our setup of makerspaces with the end in mind. Our goal is to engage young children in these spaces in interactions with interesting materials, tools, and attachments in order to build their identities and develop their capacities for multiple ways of knowing and deep thinking; improve potential for representation of their thoughts, feelings, and perceptions; and offer opportunities to enact creativity, imagination, and flexible thinking (Eckhoff 2017).

The first step in planning a new makerspace is identifying its purpose, which is related to growing the identities of our young makers (artists, collagists, builders, sculptors, performers, inventors, weavers, storytellers, and writers). Your purpose may be based on a learning practice you want to focus on, a characteristic of the maker mindset, or a current curricular or social-emotional learning goal. You know what your children need and what their interests are, so you are the best person to determine your goals. We provide examples of our goals to inspire you and give you ideas, but possibilities are limited only by your imagination and resources.

A makerspace to build and make with performance materials: 1. Inspiration and support (sign, book) 2. Main material (wood) 3. Loose parts (moss, mulch, acorns, stones, and other natural items) 4. Tools and attachments (scissors, glue sticks, liquid glue)

The purpose of the makerspace shown here is to grow our children's performer identities as they develop a character, focusing on details. Josveen is imagining a character he can make with the open-ended nature materials.

INSPIRATION AND SUPPORT

The next step is to provide inspiration and support toward the achievement of your goal. Our goal in this section is to provide specific inspirations for you as you design productive makerspaces to ignite your children's imaginations. Each chapter includes a sign for you to post in your makerspace featuring photos of materials and open-ended questions to inspire the children. Feel free to visit www.storymakers .us to download a copy of the signs for use in your makerspaces.

Sources of inspiration include the following:

- an invitation to explore the materials
- a shared read-aloud
- a new and interesting material
- a focus lesson
- guiding questions asked or posted

The goal is to ignite children's imaginations, encourage curiosity, and provoke wonderings. For this makerspace we recommend the book *Dress Like a Girl* by Patricia Toht and a sign inviting, "What character can you imagine designing with nature materials?"

Sometimes a form of support is the best inspiration. Supports include the following:

- an anchor chart displaying specific steps for using a new tool or technique, supported by visuals (Anchor charts "are charts that you create collaboratively with the students during focus lessons to anchor their thinking" [Compton and Thompson 2018, 20].)
- guiding questions that prompt student explorations across disciplines (STREAM)
- models or photographs of other children's projects or stories created in that makerspace
- fiction and nonfiction books with illustrations that can serve as models or examples

Josveen is curious about the moss. He is studying it and noticing its properties.

We offer different examples of inspiration and support in each chapter so that you will have an array of possibilities for inspiring your children.

MAIN MATERIALS

The main material is the first material you choose. In most makerspaces it serves as the base for playing and making. In the highlighted makerspace, the main material was wood craft sticks, which served as the base for the puppet design.

We provide examples of different main materials used in the variety of makerspaces set up in each chapter. The photos show how a main material might be used to accomplish learning goals in each space and what main materials might be found in each makerspace. The following chart lists some basics to begin the transformation of your current play areas:

Common Makerspace Materials that You May Have on Hand

Makerspace	Common Main Materials
Arts	Paper (watercolor, construction, copy, card stock)
Collage	Felt, construction paper, scrapbook paper, large photos, placemats
Construction	Wood blocks, cardboard brick blocks
Sculpture	Playdough
Performance	Wood craft sticks, clothespins, cardboard, paper, fabric, scarves, felt
Small World	Sand, water, dried beans, dried rice
Fiber Arts	Yarn, ribbon, fabric

Main materials from arts makerspaces

Main materials from collage makerspaces

Main materials from construction makerspaces

Main materials from sculpture makerspaces

Main materials from performance makerspaces

Main materials from small world makerspaces

Main materials from fiber arts makerspaces

LOOSE PARTS

We have lots of different categories for loose parts. Selecting a particular category of loose parts enables children to notice and more easily make connections to textures, balance, colors, forms, functions, and innovations of that type of loose part. Providing many possibilities within one category invites children to go deeper with their learning about the material and its properties and uses. With each unit we select a specific category of materials; we therefore suggest sending a letter to children's families as needed throughout the year to stock or replenish your makerspace resources (see appendix A).

We use loose parts to complexify, enhance beauty, and make thinking visible in makerspaces. The categories of loose parts we use are

- nature objects,
- wood,
- paper,
- textile,
- plastic,
- glass, and
- metal.

Nature and wood loose parts

Wood loose parts

WHAT COLLAGES DO YOU
— IMAGINE —
MAKING with PAPER?

Paper loose parts

Textile loose parts

Plastic loose parts

Glass loose parts

Metal loose parts

Organization and Aesthetics

The loose parts storage in clear containers from the atelier at Kinderoo Children's Academy in Ocala, Florida, is not only beautiful but also allows easy access for teachers to imagine possibilities for the designing of beautiful makerspaces.

Loose Parts List

Nature	Wood	Paper / Cardboard	Plastic	Metal / Reflective	Textiles	Glass
acorns	clothespins	cardboard	acetate shapes	air ducts	beanbags	doorknobs
bark	corks	mailing	bag clips	aluminum	blankets	gems
clam shells	golf tees	tubes	balloons	canning jar	burlap	glass beads
coconut shells	matchsticks	envelopes	beverage caps	lids	cotton balls	magnifying
driftwood	palettes	magazines	bingo chips	aluminum foil	doilies	glass
feathers	wood chips	manila folders	buttons	binder rings	embroidery	marbles
flower petals	wood cookies	newspaper	CD cases	clips	thread/	mirrors
flowers	wood craft	old cards	cellophane	bottle caps	string	mosaic tiles
(seasonal)	sticks	paper egg	coffee pods	brad fasteners	fabric strips	prisms
helicopter pods	wood doll pins	cartons	color paddles	bread ties	felt	sea glass
leaves	wood flooring	paper towels	curtain rings	circuit boards	flannel	window
logs	tiles	paper tubes	dice	keys	lace	blocks
moss	wood knobs	sticky notes	dominoes	metal screen	pom-poms	
nests	wood spools	tissue boxes	drink stirrers	Mylar	ribbon	
nuts		tissue paper	glow sticks	nails	rope	
pine cones			grocery bags	nuts, bolts,	scarves	
pumpkins/			gutters	and washers	stretchy	
gourds			(ramps)	paper clips	bands	
rocks/pebbles/			hair rollers	pipe cleaners	tarps	
stones			marker caps	screws	twine	
sea glass			math manipu	silverware	wool	
seashells			latives	soda tabs	yarn	
seeds			old film rolls	springs		
sponges			packing	watch parts		
sticks/			bubbles			
branches			ping-pong			
straw			balls			
vines			plastic beads			
walnut halves			and			
wood cookies			necklaces			
			plastic cups			
			plumbing			
			connectors			
			pony beads			
			pool noodles			
			PVC piping			
			straws			
			tape rolls			
			(empty)			
			thread spools			
			(empty)			

TOOLS AND ATTACHMENTS

Tools are items used to manipulate materials. Common tools in our makerspaces include the following:

- scissors
- straightedges or rulers

Attachments are connectors that enable children to attach two or more objects—typically loose parts—together during their making. Typical attachments include the following:

- glue
- tape
- wire
- binder and paper clips
- pipe cleaners
- string/twine

We list specific tools and attachments for each makerspace and suggest brand names of specific tools and attachments that we have found to be reliable and useful. This section also includes safety tips as appropriate.

The "Imagine" section of our Maker Cycle and of each chapter gets children's imaginations engaged. Now let's start playing and making!

Spaces for Playing and Making

This section provides a documentation story from the highlighted makerspace. Each story emphasizes the purpose for the makerspace, an explanation of how a child enacted the learning practices as they went through the Maker Cycle, and photos capturing it all. We then show pictures of many different materials, tools, and attachments and their uses in the featured makerspaces. One photograph per chapter features the development of social-emotional efficacy in the makerspace and is captioned "Making a Mark."

Here is your first documentation story of the power of the everyday materials and loose parts the children collected and their effects on the learning of these young makers.

It was a busy day in this public school prekindergarten classroom, with many makerspaces to choose from. As we traveled from makerspace to makerspace, the students were engaged, intrigued, interactive, and collaborative in their playing and making. In the arts makerspace, the children investigated circles, using different circular loose parts as inspiration.

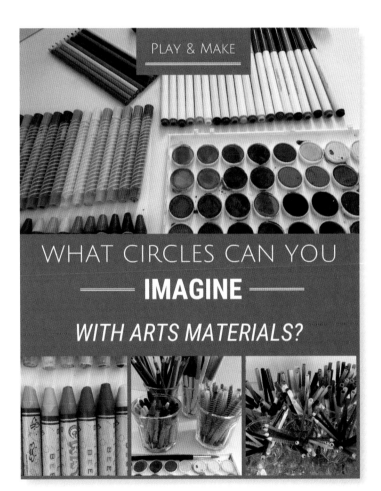

The children were invited to play and make with circles in the arts makerspace.

Hunter is curious and stacks the plastic lids.

Hunter studies the materials as he begins to tinker.

After tinkering with the materials, Hunter uses paint to play with circles.

When new materials are introduced, children often tinker, mess around, and stack and dump (literally!) the new materials. They need to figure out each material's form and function before they can start making something. On this day Hunter was most curious about the plastic lids he had discovered in the collage makerspace, where the children were using plastic loose parts to make their collages. "Why are these here? What are these for?" Hunter had never considered the possibility of using plastic lids for playing and making. He decided he wanted to paint the plastic lids. He took them to the arts makerspace, creating an opportunity for cross-disciplinary learning.

Hunter made several attempts to get the paint to stick to the plastic before figuring out that he needed the paint to be thick, with very little water added. Finally, success! He loved his new painting and decided to give it to his mom for her birthday, after it dried.

This painting made the perfect birthday gift for Hunter's mom, showing his talents as an artist and maker.

Below are the observable indicators of enactment of the learning practices during this learning engagement in the arts makerspace.

Documenting Learning in a Makerspace

Learning Practices that Lead to the Development of a Maker Mindset	Indicators of Learning through Enactment of the Practices
Inquire	• Hunter was curious about why there were bottle caps in the makerspace. He asked, "Why are these here? What are these for?"
Tinker	• Hunter stacked and played with the bottle caps, trying to get them to balance.
Seek and Share Resources	• Hunter used the materials (bottle caps) as a resource to help him figure out the properties of paint and how to use tools to paint surfaces. He shared his new knowledge during his maker talk.
Hack and Repurpose	• The bottle cap was hacked and repurposed as a painting tool used to make circles.
Express Intent	• Hunter said he wanted to "make a lot of circles."
Develop Fluency	• The longer Hunter stuck to it and tried to figure out how to get the paint to stick to the lids, the more fluent he became.
Simplify to Complexify	• Hunter combined two simple materials (plastic bottle caps and paint) to create opportunities for perseverance, complex thinking, and growing his identity as an artist.

More Spaces to Inspire Your Making

This section provides additional pictures of different main materials and loose parts used in the highlighted makerspace. It's an opportunity for you to get inspired with the variety of possibilities and ideas!

Making a Mark by organizing and sorting materials to make it easier for classmates and friends to find and use materials

Sharing Our Thinking

In each chapter we share a lesson that you might like to try out in your makerspace.

FOCUS LESSON FOR MATERIALS BROUGHT FROM HOME

Objective: Children will engage their imaginations by wondering, collecting, exploring, and organizing materials.

MATERIALS

- letter home
- bags for treasures
- large pieces of construction paper or white paper, or cookie trays, or any container for loose parts (we used individual plastic cereal containers from the cafeteria)
- "What Makers Do" and/or "What Is a Maker?" anchor chart drawn on chart paper
- markers
- camera for documentation
- your own bag filled with three to five loose parts and found materials

Focus and Explore

Connect: *"Good morning, makers! Do you remember yesterday when _____ shared what materials she used in her playing and making? She made me curious about materials. I wondered about what new materials we could place in our makerspaces. I am always curious about new materials and what I can make using those materials."* Give the children an opportunity to share their wonderings about materials. *"So today we will engage our imaginations by thinking about what interesting materials we may be able to find at home to add to our makerspaces for playing and making."*

Teach: *"Guess what, makers? Makers have eyes to notice and observe their surroundings. Do you know what that means?"* Give children an opportunity to think and share while reflecting on the "What Is a Maker?" anchor chart and charting their words. *"Yes, makers use their eyes to find and look closely at things. This is a wonderful feature of what makes us all makers. Now let's discuss what makers can do."* Reveal new anchor chart and highlight how makers wonder. *"Let's practice wondering by observing and imagining what we can make."* Pull out a loose part from your treasure bag. *"Look what I found when I took a walk in my neighborhood!"* Pull a rock out of the bag. *"A rock! What do you notice about this rock?"* Give children a chance to notice characteristics, forms, and functions (hard, brown, smooth). *"Makers also listen and learn from other makers to imagine new ideas and what they can make with materials. I wonder how we could use this rock in our makerspaces. Everybody, close your eyes. Think about how you would use this rock when you're playing and making. Think, think, think."* Give some time for thinking. *"Turn to your partner (or someone next to you) and share how you would use it in an idea or a project or a story."* Allow time for them to share ideas with one another.

Continue to pull items out of your bag and talk about them, naming your observations and noticings and possibilities of what you could make with them. (For example, *"I'm noticing that this stick is brown. And it can break in half."* Break it. *"Oh,*

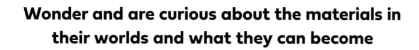

What Makers Do

Wonder and are curious about the materials in their worlds and what they can become

Learn from other makers to imagine new ideas

Use hands and tools to draw, assemble, build, sculpt, perform, invent, and stitch

Share ideas, projects, stories, and thinking

A Maker Is an . . .

artist, collagist, builder, sculptor, performer, inventor, weaver, storyteller, and writer!

"What Makers Do" anchor chart

I have an idea. These two pieces of my stick can be walls of my tent in my story." Give the children time to share how they might use the materials and what they notice about them.

Active Involvement: "*I had fun sharing my materials with you. You are each going to get a chance to gather treasures for your bag. You are going to get a bag just like this to take home! When you take your bags home, you and your families can wonder about and notice the treasures in your house and in your backyard and in your neighborhood, and put them in your bags. You are going to look for bits and pieces that you want to use in our makerspaces.*" Refer to the What Makers Do chart and explain that makers wonder and are curious about the materials in their world and what they can become.

"*What are you imagining you will collect on your treasure hunt?*" Have the children share with their neighbors about the materials they are thinking about. As they do that, document what materials they want to explore and what materials or makerspaces they are going to use.

Imagine

Ask children to pause and think about what materials they want to explore today. Record their ideas on the Class at a Glance form to document frequency in use of materials and ideas (see appendix C).

Play and Make

Document the learning practices children exhibit while making by taking pictures and dictation and using the Learning Practices Documentation form (see appendix B). This form may help you identify the enactment of the learning practices as you observe your children playing and making. An easy place to start is identifying children's inquiries as they express curiosity, show excitement, and ask questions.

Share

Select a child who used simple, everyday materials to give a maker talk. Have the child gather all materials and tools prior to the maker talk, or take a photo of the project. During the talk, prompt the child with questions, such as "This is a picture of what you have been making. Can you tell us about the materials you used?" or "Can you point to the parts of your construction (or sculpture, collage, and so on) and tell us how you made it?"

SUGGESTED BOOKS TO INSPIRE MAKERS

We love using books to inspire our makers! Each chapter has a list of recommended children's books relevant to the featured makerspace. Here are books about making and makers that you can use with any of your makerspaces:

Adaptations for Makers with Special Rights

If you have nonverbal children, provide them with options during their sharing. You could narrate the processes, projects, or stories as they point to different materials to ensure that they get to participate in maker talks.

Rosie Revere, Engineer by Andrea Beaty

What If . . . by Samantha Berger

Papa's Mechanical Fish by Candace Fleming

Be a Maker by Katey Howes

Have Fun, Molly Lou Melon by Patty Lovell

Little Robot Alone by Patricia MacLachlan and Emily MacLachlan Charest

Little Engineers by Haig Norian

Anywhere Artist by Nikki Slade Robinson

The Most Magnificent Thing by Ashley Spires

Made by Maxine by Ruth Spiro

With My Hands: Poems about Making Things by Amy Ludwig VanDerwater

What Do You Do with an Idea? by Kobi Yamada

Next Steps in Transforming Spaces

By creating intentional makerspaces for playing and making where children enact the learning practices of the maker movement, you are building a maker mindset in your young makers. As you transform your play areas to makerspaces and grow comfortable introducing new or different materials, make sure your makerspaces are developing your makers' mindsets. In this section of each chapter, we provide examples of how the learning practices build a maker mindset and pose questions for you to consider with your colleagues as you reflect on the children's growth. The Learning Practices Documentation form (appendix B) will help you document the enactment of learning practices. For example, you may notice your children using the read-aloud books as inspiration. Children also use one another and the materials to generate ideas. Note these behaviors under "Seek and Share Resources" on the form. Seeking resources builds a growth mindset as children learn that they can be successful by getting help and seeking resources.

Take a moment to have a maker talk with your colleagues to share, collaborate, and consider next steps in the transformation of your makerspaces.

- Examine the Learning Practices Documentation form. Discuss it with your colleagues. How will you use it to document the enactment of the learning practices in your children?
- What is the first space you plan to transform? What ideas do you have? How can your colleagues support you as you think it through and get started?
- How will you organize your loose parts for your makerspace? What containers have worked for you?
- What STREAM learning connections would you like to emphasize that would guide your language prompts and selection of materials, loose parts, tools, and attachments?

WHAT CAN YOU IMAGINE

MAKING

WITH THESE ART MATERIALS?

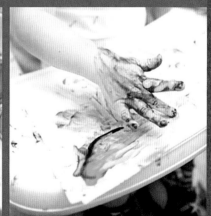

An invitation for children to imagine, play,
and make in the arts makerspace

CHAPTER 2

Arts Makerspaces

ART

Touching the paper and tinkering with lines,
I'm inspired to make colorful designs.
With brushes, I spill, mix, and splatter.
My canvas tells stories that truly matter.

Stories to Inspire Making

Excitement grew as the children noticed some interesting new materials in the arts makerspace. It was the first time they had seen black construction paper as a main material. There was also a single piece of white chart paper. "What's that for?" Oil pastels of varying colors and shades, from "the sky" to "a worm," had been arranged in an aesthetically pleasing color spectrum, keeping the color families together. These simple new materials would lead to big discoveries: "That's my skin color. And that one is your skin color." The black paper will be used for playing and making with the oil pastels: "Hey. Black don't show up." The blank white paper will be filled with the children's words defining one of the elements of art, lines. (For more on the elements of art, see appendix D.) Inspired by the children's book *When a Line Bends . . . a Shape Begins* by Rhonda Gowler Greene, the children suggest creative expressions for the lines they discover in the illustrations: ant lines (- - - -), caterpillar lines (∿∿), and a fishing pole line (⌒). Their words, along with vocabulary that aligns with the study of lines, will be written on the chart paper to remind them of the types of lines they can include in their art making.

Their imaginations are engaged, and they can't wait to play by etching lines in the oil pastels on black paper. Black paper is suggested for etching with pastels because it is more likely to show the layers of colors. The children are playing with the medium and the colors: "It smears!" "Look at my hand! It's green!" "I can layer the colors?" Indeed, you can. They begin by layering two colors, remarking about how smoothly the pastels go on the paper, "like ice cream." They start etching lines

The materials inspire our young artists.

Stephanie had pink under red when she etched.

Stephanie explores what happens when pink is layered over yellow.

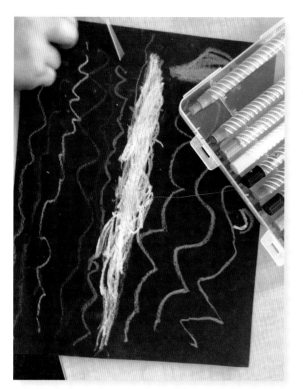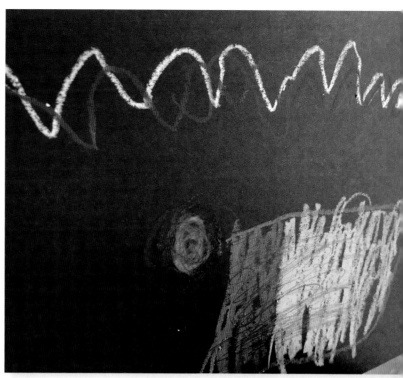

Experimenting with curved lines, spiral lines, zigzags, and more

with their fingernails, as described by Ann Pelo (2017), but figure out a better way, using a paper clip tool they develop for playing and making. The results of playing with lines, etching, and oil pastels reflect only a fraction of what the children learned, discovered, thought about, experimented with, and talked about. The children are becoming artists as they pay attention to and wonder about the forms and functions of the materials found in the arts makerspace.

The makers' processes, combined with their products, display the learning practices of the maker movement in action and provide evidence that "materials have the ability to support children in making new connections with themselves, others, and the ever-changing world around them" (Penfold 2019).

Why Is Arts the First Makerspace to Introduce to Children?

Every educational space for young children, whether informal or formal, is likely to have an area that contains some sort of tools and materials for art. What art materials do you have access to now? Crayons? Pencils? Paper? Paints? You see, you're already ready to begin designing and setting up an arts makerspace!

Also, because art "embraces nearly every experience in the classroom, from building with blocks to creating a composition on the light table," it is a great place to start transforming typical areas into makerspaces (Massey 2017, 8). As art is represented in a two-dimensional form, it can serve as the foundation for all other spaces. We will grow our makerspaces from two-dimensional (arts) to three-dimensional (collage), from three-dimensional solids (construction) to three-dimensional solids with space (sculpture) to three-dimensional solids with space and movement (performance), to the development of small worlds to house all that has been learned, and finally back to arts (fiber) to weave all the lessons together in collaboration and community.

Remaking an Art Area into an Arts Makerspace

We initially worked with our teachers to include art as one of the languages of StoryMaking, in alignment with Loris Malaguzzi's Hundred Languages of Reggio Emilia. As children used art mediums to represent their unique stories, we noticed that the paintings and other artistic representations did not all look alike. And the art was used to communicate stories. We wanted to grow the possibilities and celebrate the children's art processes and products as unique ways for them to continue to share their stories, but also to represent and communicate their ideas, projects, and thinking. In transforming our art areas into makerspaces, we focused on the children's artistic and aesthetic development while honoring their unique interpretations, perspectives, and histories.

Artistic development here includes a celebration of both process art, where "the emphasis is on the process of creating, not on the end result. . . . The child is free to explore the materials, free to construct her own interpretations, free to express herself" (Rucci 2016, 9), and product art, where there are "structured and focused activities that aim to produce a particular outcome," such as increased knowledge about the elements of art, famous artists, and techniques (Penfold 2019). There is a place for both process and product art in the arts makerspace. Additionally, aesthetics development, with a focus on finding beauty in the world and making our world more beautiful with the arts, introduces the children to new ways of knowing and of representing thinking, and offers them opportunities to become mindful observers. Research demonstrates that "every human being has the potential to develop sensitivity to what is beautiful" (Feeney and Moravcik 1987, 15).

Although art spaces often contain materials and tools, they may lack intention, inspiration, support, and materials that invite discovery and experimentation.

The remaking of an art area to an arts makerspace starts with intentional planning, selecting an element of art on which to focus (color, line, shape, texture, space, design), and an artist whose work can inspire and support the learning goals. Next, select your materials and tools. Below we provide some ideas of what you need to start transforming your art area to an arts makerspace.

Organization/ Aesthetics

Arranging items by color allows for easy access and cleanup. For example, keep all green markers together and all orange markers together. Arranging mediums (pastels, markers, crayons, paints) by color family also creates a warm or cool color spectrum that is pleasing to the eye and easier to keep organized.

Designing Your First Arts Makerspace

Inspiration	• *Sky Color* by Peter H. Reynolds, or other children's books about art or artists or with beautiful illustrations (e.g., *The Dot, Ish, Henri's Scissors*); read and set out copies to inspire children in the elements of art • Makerspace sign to encourage making ("What art elements do you imagine using to make something beautiful?" or "What can you imagine making with these art materials?") • Focus lesson on one of the elements of art, an artist, or a new art material or technique; for an example, see the lesson featured at the beginning of this chapter, which is also included at the end of this chapter
Main Materials	• Paper (construction, copy, card stock, whatever you already have), crayons, pencils, markers, paints
Loose Parts	• Not necessary, but items can be used to show examples of subtleties in line, color, shape, texture, and design
Tools and Attachments	• Paintbrushes, cups or palettes for mixing paints, craft sticks to stir and mix, tape to adhere paintings in place on the table

Before and after of the transformation from art area to emerging arts makerspace

After children have had an opportunity to play and make with the art materials, consider next steps in your makerspace. Identify where your students are on the continuum below. If they are still figuring out the form and function of a material or tool, the next step might be providing extra time and practice so they become more competent in its uses and applications. If your students are investigating more complex mediums (pastels, paints) and using them with fluency, you might introduce them to new techniques or move to digital applications and higher-tech tools and materials. Use the continuum to guide your next steps as you introduce children to a wider range of possibilities in the arts makerspace.

Maker's Continuum of Playing and Making for Art

Arts and Crafts

High Tech

Children select a medium or material to investigate as they focus on process (exploration, discovery), product (color, line, shape, texture, space, design), or aesthetics (how to make it beautiful). They explore the forms and functions of art materials (crayons, colored pencils, markers, finger paint) and tools (paintbrushes, stir sticks). Once they've figured out the uses of each of the materials available, they develop fluency with techniques and mediums.

Children work with more complex materials and tools, such as watercolors, chalk pastels, oil pastels, and thin paintbrushes for details, and begin to play, make, and innovate with processes and products, such as using lines to express importance and colors to represent feelings. They use ideas and examples of famous art to inspire, replicate, and innovate with techniques, elements, and materials represented in the artists' works.

Children make and use digital tools (Makey Makey, Doodlecast, Mixerpiece) to develop a deep understanding of what qualifies as art, how to combine elements to create art, and more. They become proficient with using, reusing, and repurposing tools as they explore art and beauty.

Adaptations for the Youngest Makers

Controlled scribbling is an introduction to drawing. As the child scribbles, you might say, "Tell me about your drawing." Help narrate the story or idea and take direction from the child.

STREAM Learning in the Arts Makerspace

Elements of the arts can be found throughout any curriculum and represented in STREAM learning. Children in the arts makerspace work in each of its domains, most specifically the arts. But our young artists use a cross-disciplinary approach to develop competence in each of the domains.

Prompts to Ensure STREAM Learning Connections

Science	Makers will do the following: • Use senses to make discoveries about lines, textures, colors, shapes, design, and space in paintings ("How did the artist use lines/color/shape to make something beautiful?" or "How can you mix colors to create new colors?") • Examine objects and make comparisons ("What do you notice about this color/shape/material/artwork?")
Technology	• Use appropriate tools (paintbrushes, stir sticks) and materials (pastels, watercolors) with greater flexibility as they create pictures to reflect their thinking, stories, ideas, and projects ("What tools do you need to make the idea/project/story that you imagine?")
Reading/Literacy	• Use sketching, drawing, and painting to express feelings and share stories/ideas ("How would you like to share your artwork or process?") • Practice with lines, forms, and shapes, becoming writers and eventually moving their scribbles to letter strings ("You are ready to take your story/idea/project to paper!")
Engineering	• Identify problems (paper is wet and ripped) and try to solve them (put in sun to dry) ("Could you tell me what is happening with your artwork/process?" "What could you do to resolve this problem?")
Arts	• Grow their identities as artists, learn the elements of art, and discover famous artists ("What or who inspired your thinking as you made your art?")
Mathematics	• Recognize and draw shapes ("What shapes did you include in your art?" "What do the shapes represent?") • Use balance, perspective, and measurement to make art ("What is the biggest/smallest/tallest object in your art?")

Imagine Making an Arts Makerspace

The purpose of the arts makerspace is to develop the identity of the artist as our young artists find meaning through creating beauty, which is made possible by developing fluency and expertise with color, shape, texture, form, space, and design. These are the elements found in every makerspace but accentuated and explicitly focused on in the arts makerspace. How to combine colors, select the proper tools, and use the materials that will best represent thinking and create beauty are goals of each of our makerspaces, but the arts makerspace specifically addresses these components.

Arts makerspace with a focus on color with watercolors: 1. Inspiration and support (*The Dot*, sign, paintings by Claude Monet) 2. Main material (watercolors, watercolor paper) 3. Loose parts (not needed) 4. Tools and attachments (paint tray palette, paintbrush, painters' tape around the watercolor paper)

Arts makerspace featuring work by Claude Monet to inspire color

INSPIRATION AND SUPPORT

This prekindergarten public school classroom had been using watercolor trays with solid watercolor pods, but we decided to try liquid watercolors because the children said their paint colors didn't match when they put them on the paper. Liquid watercolors have deep and robust colors. As suggested by Ann Pelo (2017) and Barbara Rucci (2016), we selected two to three colors, with each palette from the same color family. We read the story *Sky Color* by Peter H. Reynolds. The character, Marisol, cannot find blue paint to paint the sky. She studies the sky and realizes that sunsets contain reds, yellows, purples, and pinks; cloudy skies are gray; and so on. We talked about using only two or three colors and how the children could play with the colors, like Marisol did. We discussed the colors in each palette, and the children walked around the makerspace to study their choices. They were inspired by Marisol and couldn't wait to choose their color palettes and get started with playing and making. We shared Reynolds's book *The Dot* to show the colors in the dot on the cover. We had similar colors in some of the palettes.

After determining which element of art we wanted to foster in our artists, we researched and selected the specific supports we needed in the area. For example, in this makerspace our focus was on the element of color, and the two books were our inspiration. We next sought renowned artists to serve as strong models in the makerspace and techniques to highlight with anchor charts, as described in the project-based approach to art. In this makerspace support provided to the children included pictures of sunsets by Claude Monet, who included reds and oranges in some of his skies (*Parliament at Sunset*) and blues and greens in other sunset skies (*San Giorgio Maggiore at Dusk*).

In this makerspace we focused on color, talking about violet and purple, yellow and orange, and green and blue. The children played with colors and tones, adding more water or more paint to change the tones of their colors.

Arts makerspace with exploration of two or three colors in the same color family

Paper is the most common main material in art at this level. For this makerspace we used liquid watercolors and 140–pound watercolor paper. We didn't want to risk the paper tearing as children added water to the vibrant colors, so we selected heavier paper.

Rucci (2016), author of *Art Workshop for Children*, recommends keeping several basic papers on hand:

- plain white paper for drawing and coloring
- lightweight (90#) watercolor paper
- sulphite paper (smooth white paper) for crayons, tempera, pastels
- heavy construction paper for painting

Although you can use many other surfaces for art, paper is a good medium for learning the elements of art. It also offers lots of options for discovery and experimentation.

Children are excited and curious when introduced to interesting art mediums. We introduce art mediums along the developmental continuum suggested by Pelo (2017). You may not have access to all of these materials, but the list can help you decide when to introduce the materials you have. Each medium, or main material, has attributes to consider when selecting your particular product. We include some brands with which we've had success as well.

- crayons: OOLY Natural Beeswax Crayons are triangular and made for small hands
- colored pencils
- markers
- finger paints
- tempera paints: Recommended for mixing and creating colors. If you're just getting started with paint, offer red, blue, yellow, and white. Start by mixing only two colors.
- watercolors: We recommend starting with liquid watercolors because the colors have depth and you can add water if they are too opaque. We like Dr. Ph. Martin's, but there are many other brands as well. If you prefer to use watercolor pods, we've enjoyed the large array of appealing colors in OOLY Lil' Paint Pods.
- chalk pastels: Recommended for developing proficiency with color.
- oil pastels: We used OOLY Oil Pastel Twisty Stix at first. Each stick is encased in plastic, so the children's hands get far less messy than when using a raw stick. They are easy for children to twist, and they work like other oil pastels.

Thick paper helps when children experiment with paint colors and water.

LOOSE PARTS

We did not add loose parts to this exploration, but generally, loose parts in the arts makerspace become tools (paintbrushes made from sticks and leaves; sponges or packing bubbles used to add texture), props (items that represent specific shapes as we study shape or mixtures that show subtle differences in color), or scaffolds toward independence (items that the children can trace to build confidence as they get started).

When children introduce loose parts to their art pieces, their art becomes collage. Considered a fine art medium, collage is the act of layering (and sometimes attaching) objects and papers to a surface to create a three-dimensional expression or idea. We will discuss how to add loose parts to art during playing and making in chapter 3, Collage Makerspaces.

Natural brushes made from sticks and leaves

TOOLS AND ATTACHMENTS

Tools in this makerspace included paintbrushes in a variety of sizes, palettes for holding the paints, and cups for holding water. Many tools are useful in the arts makerspace. Below are some reminders of what you may already have:

- electric pencil sharpener
- easel
- craft sticks (mixing and moving paints)
- hand lens (close study of details in paintings or other works of art)
- mirrors (reflect the underside of items and can add light and reflection to details of a subject being drawn or painted)
- erasers
- paintbrushes (large brushes for spreading paint and finer brushes for detail work; Rucci recommends First Impressions brushes, round #8 and #10, and IKEA's paintbrushes [2016, 25])

For attachments in this makerspace, we used a good idea suggested by Rucci (2016) and taped the borders of the paintings to create the look of a natural frame when they're dry. Painter's tape works the best. Other attachments used in the arts makerspace include

- tape to repair tears and rips, and
- clips or clothespins for hanging and displaying.

Adaptations for Makers with Special Rights

Easels emphasize movement, and large easels and tabletop easels can serve the same purpose. Select easels that meet the needs of students who either need to sit or stand.

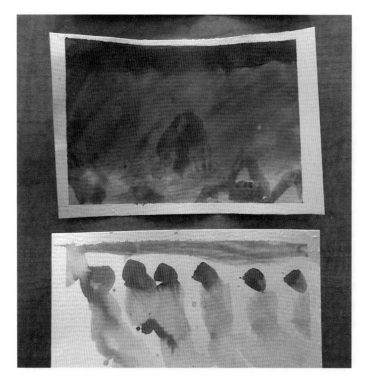

A border of tape during watercolor painting secures the work surface and forms a simple frame when removed after paintings are dry. ("Creatures living in the ocean" and "All my friends at the sunset")

Organization/ Aesthetics

If you are using watercolors, you will need containers of water, which are often spilled. Secure the water cups to the table or surface with adhesive putty, or put water in metal muffin tins for greater stability.

Spaces for Playing and Making

Each time we visited a prekindergarten public school classroom throughout the year, we tried to bring an interesting new material or idea with us. Integrated classrooms have both typically developing students and students who have special needs, so there are many developmental levels within one group. We noticed that many of the children liked coloring with crayons and some had started making circles out of their scribbles. Circles are one of the first shapes that children experiment with, so we set up a makerspace where students could experiment, play, and make with circles (Pelo 2017 ; Topal and Gandini 1999). We set up the makerspace while the children were at lunch, and they were so excited when they returned to find new and interesting materials alongside their old favorites, crayons.

There were several inspirations for the children in this makerspace. The question posed on the sign—"What circles do you imagine making with crayons?"—set the goal of exploring their identities as artists and studying the element of shape as they played and made with circles. We posted copies of several of Wassily Kandinsky's circle paintings so the children could study the circle techniques of a famous artist to support their learning. The main materials were crayons and simple white card stock.

We added circular metal loose parts and other everyday materials as an inspiration to show different sizes of circles. We talked about the loose parts and what circular loose parts the children might have at home (pennies, lids, mirrors, bobbins, thimbles, beads, bottle caps, washers).

We did not use additional tools or attachments in this makerspace.

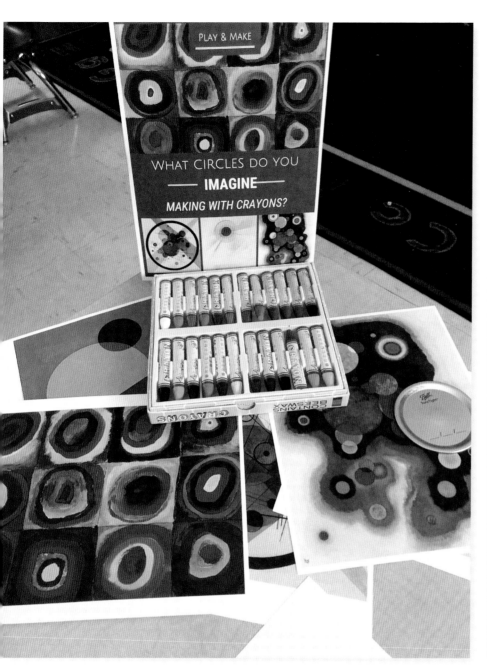

Study of circles with crayons

Metal loose parts for circle study

The children couldn't wait to get started! Some needed the additional scaffolding of Kandinsky's artwork. Even though they used the artwork for inspiration, each child selected different colors, spaces, and designs, thus ensuring unique outcomes.

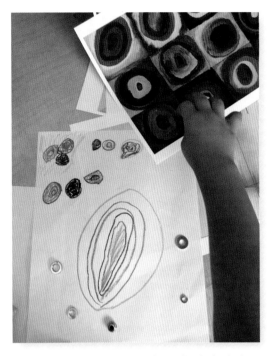 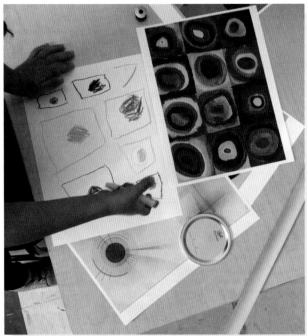

Different interpretations of Kandinsky's circles

Some children used the loose parts to get started. They placed the smaller loose parts inside their large circles and traced the objects.

Isidro placed some of the metal washers on a mirror. He arranged them and rearranged them. He tinkered for quite a while, getting them just right. As soon as they were the way he had imagined them, he began to draw circles in a straight line across his paper. He selected his colors carefully. His intent was to make circles, each in a different color, across the top of his page, which later became the bottom of his art. Isidro was curious about the new crayons and wanted to try each of the colors.

Loose parts scaffold the children's circle making.

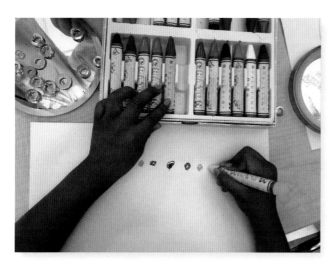

Isidro makes a row of circles, experimenting with colors.

He left for a while and went to play in another makerspace. Then he came back. When he returned, he added some more circles.

Isidro uses loose parts to trace circles.

First he added the red circles at the bottom of his page. Then he traced some metal props to make bigger circles. The biggest circle of all he drew himself. And then he added even more circles! He was developing fluency with drawing circles by practicing and using scaffolds (loose parts) to help him.

Isidro hacked and repurposed his picture by turning it upside down. "The circles are still circles!" He liked it that way better. He was very happy when he finished his circle drawing.

Below are observable indicators of enactment of the learning practices during this learning engagement in the arts makerspace.

Documenting Learning in the Arts Makerspace

Learning Practices that Lead to the Development of a Maker Mindset	Indicators of Learning through Enactment of the Practices
Inquire	• Isidro was curious about the new crayons and wanted to try out each of the colors. He was willing to try out materials in new ways and for new purposes.
Tinker	• Isidro arranged and rearranged the loose parts until they represented his conception of his representation.
Seek and Share Resources	• Isidro walked around the classroom and looked for additional circular loose parts to match his thinking. Eventually he used them to make his thinking visible in the artwork that he shared.
Hack and Repurpose	• Isidro changed his original thinking by turning his paper upside down.
Express Intent	• Isidro selected his colors carefully. He said he wanted to make circles, each in a different color, across the top of his page. He followed through on his plan.
Develop Fluency	• Isidro drew many circles, at first tracing the loose parts and then drawing circles on his own. With practice he developed fluency in drawing circles.
Simplify to Complexify	• Isidro's picture matched his thinking, and he was very pleased with his process and product. He took simple materials and created a picture that was meaningful to him and a complex representation of his thinking.

More Arts Makerspaces to Inspire Your Making

If you have not worked with the elements of art as your inspiration in the past, we want you to feel confident as you plan your arts makerspace and its accompanying components. See appendix D for more information on the elements. Below are pictures of some of the arts makerspaces we have set up, using the elements of art and renowned artists as our starting points.

Exploration of shape with colored pencils

Exploration of design with markers, using Andy Warhol's soup cans as inspiration, and tinkering with playdough containers

Exploration of color with watercolor paints and works by Henri Matisse

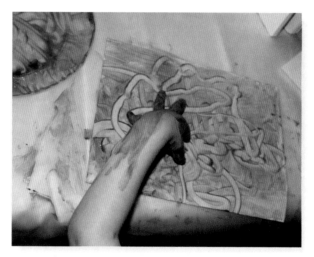

Exploration of texture with finger paints and works by Claude Monet

Exploration of color with paint on foil and works by Claude Monet

Exploration of lines with chalk pastels and works by Vincent van Gogh

Exploration of space with Doodlecast digital drawing

Making a Mark by using art to show what love looks like as the JK3 children at the Episcopal School of Knoxville demonstrate acts of kindness.

Play and Make

Give the children plenty of time to experiment, play, and make lines with the new materials. They will want to practice using different colors and finding tools to make different sorts and sizes of lines. Observe the children and notice if they are playing around with lots of different colors or trying out many different lines. Are they investigating the materials and their affordances? If so, they are thinking with their hands, or tinkering. Are they using common materials for new purposes, for example, using everyday items to carve lines (toothpicks, skewers, paper clips)? If so, they are hacking and repurposing. Do you notice that they are accomplishing the lines they imagined more easily with practice? They are developing fluency.

Share

Find a child who made lines with the oil pastels to share with the group in a maker talk to inspire future makers in the arts makerspace. Ask the children to explain and describe what they made and how they made it. Ask questions like "What did you make?" and "How did you make it?"

SUGGESTED BOOKS TO INSPIRE MAKERS WITH THE ARTS

Sometimes it's difficult to come up with new ideas and book recommendations. Choose books that highlight art elements and famous artists. These are some of the children's books we've used in focus lessons and to inspire our children in the arts makerspace:

I'm Not Just a Scribble by Diane Alber
Splatter by Diane Alber
The Crayon Man: The True Story of the Invention of Crayola Crayons
    by Natascha Biebow
The Line by Paula Bossio
Maybe Something Beautiful: How Art Transformed a Neighborhood
    by F. Isabel Campoy and Theresa Howell
Swatch: The Girl Who Loved Color by Julia Denos
Drawn Together by Minh Lê
Louise Loves Art by Kelly Light
Niko Draws a Feeling by Bob Raczka
Ish by Peter H. Reynolds
Sky Color by Peter H. Reynolds
I Feel Teal by Lauren Rille
Beautiful Oops! by Barney Saltzberg
Look! Look! Look! by Nancy Elizabeth Wallace
Uncle Andy's: A Faabbbulous Visit with Andy Warhol by James Warhola
Lines That Wiggle by Candace Whitman

These are the artists we use as inspiration:

Vincent's Colors by Vincent van Gogh (There are a lot of van Gogh kid books, but
    this is our favorite.)
Blue and Other Colors with Henri Matisse
A Blue Butterfly: A Story about Claude Monet by Bijou Le Tord

Next Steps in Transforming Spaces

By creating an intentional arts makerspace for playing and making with the art
elements and famous artworks, celebrating both process and products, you are
building a maker mindset in your young artists. As you feel comfortable introducing the different art mediums you have and using loose parts to scaffold and inspire, observe the children and watch for the characteristics of a maker mindset
emerging in their interactions with one another and the materials. For example, do
you notice children becoming more confident in their choices and techniques as
they practice and improve? They are developing fluency and building their growth
mindset. Do you see evidence of increased sharing materials, taking turns using
them, and developing friendships? They are developing social-emotional efficacy
through sharing and collaborating.

- What learning practices have you observed in children as they play and make
  in the arts makerspace? How are these behaviors connected to the maker
  mindset?
- Ask your children, "What have you learned about becoming a maker? What
  new skills do you have as an artist?" Reflect on how their responses are connected to the maker mindset.
- What art materials do your children use most often and for the longest periods of time in the makerspace? How can you tweak those materials to spark
  wonder?
- What new materials do you imagine introducing to the arts makerspace? What
  ideas do your colleagues have about their materials?
- Which elements of art do you feel comfortable teaching? Uncomfortable? Why
  do you think you feel this way? What can you do to gain confidence?

WHAT CAN YOU
— IMAGINE —
MAKING with
COLLAGE MATERIALS?

An invitation for children to imagine, play, and make in the collage makerspace

CHAPTER 3

Collage Makerspaces

A collection of scraps now catches my eye.
These everyday pieces become my supplies.
Assembling treasures all over the floor,
My art takes shape, my creativity soars!

Stories to Inspire Making

Fall was in the air, and emerald-green leaves with hints of the changing season invited the children to explore new nature materials in a pop-up makerspace at The Muse Knoxville museum. The group entered a collage makerspace filled with leaves of varying sizes, shapes, and textures, ready to explore the possibilities by arranging and connecting the fresh, ripe seed pods and bushy moss to make what they imagined. Children of different ages couldn't wait to get their hands on the materials. Materials draw us in and remind us of memories, give us new ideas, and move our thinking forward. For one child, the spiky fern sections conjured images of a soldier going on a hunt. Another child used the same material to give flight to her beloved owl creation and provided a branch where her creature could perch.

An invitation for children to explore nature materials and loose parts in a collage makerspace

Lincoln imagined, played, and made the ferns into a soldier going on a hunt and then shared his story, which his father wrote down.

Dana imagined and made wings and a branch with the fern materials.

Cutting, shaping, and attaching these materials breathed life into the images the children made and allowed them to communicate the story or information they had woven together in their nature collages. Once again, the materials were in a relationship with the children during tinkering and making with the three-dimensional medium, collage.

Why Is Collage the Next Makerspace to Introduce to Children?

As children enact their knowledge of the art elements learned in the arts makerspace, they create beautiful processes and two-dimensional products that evidence knowledge of lines, shapes, textures, spaces, colors, and design. When our young artists start adding loose parts and layers to their art, it becomes a collage. Collage—the act of layering (and sometimes attaching) objects and papers to a surface to create a three-dimensional expression or idea, is a natural next level of complexity in their maker abilities. Collagists consider each of the elements of art as they make their collages. The collage makerspace takes the two-dimensional arts makerspace to the next level by adding another dimension. Collage is three-dimensional, with the addition of loose parts.

Designing a Collage Makerspace

The collage makerspace was initially an extension to our art area, as we noticed the children naturally created collages when they added loose parts to their drawings and paintings, moving from two-dimensional works to three-dimensional. Even though collage could look like a transformation of the arts makerspace, we wanted to retain and celebrate the arts makerspace, with its emphasis on recognizing and making beauty and its focus on the elements of art in a two-dimensional format. We thus recommend adding collage as a new makerspace.

Although most classrooms and other learning environments, informal and formal, do not have a collage area, this inexpensive makerspace inspires curiosity, does not take up a lot of space, and can be easily changed to maintain interest and lead to increased skills and capacity for our makers. It also demonstrates the enactment of the learning practices of the maker movement.

The collage makerspace invites children to place and arrange materials and loose parts to represent their imaginings and thinking. "Collage is a layering of thoughts and ideas as well as of paper, fabric, glue, and paint. . . . Collages might even be considered biographies of the lives of the artists—or even as historical artifacts themselves" (Brommer 1994, 9). The following list will help you design and set up your first collage makerspace with materials you may already have.

Designing Your First Collage Makerspace

Inspiration	• Children's books that focus on or use collages in their illustrations (books by Lois Ehlert, such as *RRRalph*, *The Scraps Book*, or *Leaf Man*, are a great place to start); read and set out copies as inspiration • Makerspace sign to encourage making ("What can you imagine making with collage materials?") • Focus lesson on how to make a collage using specific materials (metal, plastic, nature, textiles). For example, the lesson featured at the end of this chapter demonstrates how to make collages using plastic.
Main Materials	• The main material serves as the base of the collage, so just about any flat-surfaced material can work. Use what you already have: paper, felt, cardboard, placemats, photos.
Loose Parts	• Small, open-ended pieces and parts that you already have, such as buttons, beads, shells, stones, coins, nuts and bolts, twigs, leaves, fabric scraps, bottle caps.
Tools and Attachments	• Scissors, small hands, tweezers • We do not typically attach loose parts to the main material, as we want to be able to reuse everything, but occasionally we use glue (fabric, sticks, Mod Podge) and tape (washi, clear).

Organization/ Aesthetics

If you have no extra space in your classroom, collage is an ideal pop-up makerspace that requires little room and few materials. Use a travel caddy or silverware trays to display the loose parts on a shelf or table.

The collage makerspace is near and dear to our hearts, as it is the first new makerspace we started in our research and investigations of how children play and make for *StoryMaking*. In the natural transition from art to collage, we observed a transformation in the children's thinking, playing, and making. We started to question and investigate the possibilities of transforming all of our typical areas into makerspaces to increase the potential for learning through playing and making and to include STREAM concepts and domains.

Start by giving the children time to play with the materials and figure out the form, function, and limits of each. We recommend starting with three to five different loose parts (for example, shells, stones, leaves, and twigs) and one base (felt). Once children have had a chance to play and make collages, introduce additional loose parts. Ten to fifteen shells or a small bag of beads are enough for a table of four to six children to play, make, and share. An overabundance of materials can create a mess and prevent opportunities for sharing and taking turns. Below is a continuum to guide your steps as you plan your collage makerspace.

Before and after of the transformation from table area to emerging collage makerspace

Arts and Crafts

High Tech

Children play with collage materials to determine form, function, and affordances prior to creating collages. They may arrange the loose parts by category (size, color, texture) during their play.

Children select a base material to use as the foundation for representing their thinking. Examples include

- paper (construction or copy paper, card stock, cardboard, scrapbook papers, photographs);
- felt;
- metal cookie sheet;
- clear contact paper; and
- placemats.

They cut, tear, and fold paper into the shapes they imagine for their collage and arrange it with other loose parts. They tinker, test, and iterate the representations of the loose parts.

Children work with more complex materials (smaller loose parts, new materials, familiar materials used in new ways), tools (small hands, tweezers, scissors), and attachments (glue sticks, liquid glue, washi tape, clear tape), if used.

They learn more complex forms and functions to make collages using a variety of loose parts, including an increased array of paper, nature materials, plastic, metal (sometimes needs to be cut with snips or wire cutters), and fabric (can be attached with needle and thread).

Children make and use high-tech tools (paper circuits) and use, reuse, and repurpose materials (bottle caps, foil, buttons, stamps) as they make collages, using found materials and recyclables in new and innovative ways.

Organization/Aesthetics

The collage makerspace has many small parts and pieces, so you'll need containers to keep them . . . contained! We have used plastic bottles with snap-on lids, fishing tackle boxes, and glass jars. We recommend containers with lids, rather than open baskets. Labeling the containers sends the message that a particular item, rather than an assortment of loose parts, goes back into that container.

STREAM Learning in the Collage Makerspace

Children use the knowledge they gained in the arts makerspace as they consider balance, space, and design in assembling their collages. They also add to their learning as their wonderings, questions, and aha moments cross disciplines and support them in creating beautiful and meaningful collages.

Prompts to Ensure STREAM Learning Connections

Science	Makers will do the following: • Examine new materials and repurpose commonly used materials into something innovative to represent thinking ("What could you use these materials for as you make your collage?") • Develop representations of familiar or imagined stories/ideas/ projects using collage materials ("What stories/ideas/projects can you imagine making with these collage materials?") • Compare which materials best represent their thinking/ imaginations ("Which material will work best as you imagine and make your collage?")
Technology	• Use appropriate tools (tweezers, fingers, scissors) to rip/tear/cut/ arrange ("What tool will work best to help you make the shapes you imagine for your collage?")
Reading/Literacy	• Use collage to communicate ideas with others ("Tell me about your collage.") • Describe objects, actions, and events represented in collage ("What story are you making with collage materials?") • Use language to express feelings ("How are you feeling as you play and make your collage?")
Engineering	• Represent thinking with a model ("What materials will best represent your thinking as you imagine your collage?") • Ask questions to identify problems ("What are you wondering about as you make your collage?") • Plan and design story/idea/project ("What materials do you intend to use as you make your collage?")
Arts	• Identify the elements of art (color, shape, line, space, design) found in the collage ("What lines/colors/shapes do you notice in your collage?")
Mathematics	• Identify patterns ("Do you notice any patterns in your collage?") • Count items ("How many loose parts did you use in your collage?") • Compare and measure ("Did you use more shells or more rocks to make your collage?") • Cut shapes to the exact size and shape desired for their collages ("What size/shape piece would fit there in your collage?")

Imagine Making a Collage Makerspace

The purpose of the collage makerspace is to develop our young collagists' identities as they make an assemblage of different forms, thus creating a new whole (Lord 1958). Children create collages that represent their thoughts, ideas, histories, and perspectives using open-ended materials, tools, and attachments. In this makerspace our collagists investigated an array of textiles, considering and experimenting with the weight, textures, forms, functions, and limits of each in representing what they imagined.

INSPIRATION AND SUPPORT

We designed a series of pop-up makerspaces hosted for the community at Clinton Public Library in Clinton, Tennessee. The children had previously attended collage makerspaces featuring nature and paper loose parts. We wanted them to explore fabric loose parts next because it is a more complex material and requires different tools to manipulate and change the shape. Anchor charts can both inspire and support, serving as a teaching tool and a reminder to children about a lesson or technique. We had introduced our collage anchor chart in a focus lesson at the opening of the collage makerspace.

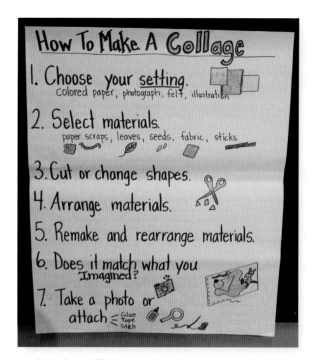

Anchor chart offering support for collage techniques

Inspiration for collage makerspace with textile loose parts

In the makerspace pictured, the anchor chart from a previous lesson served as a supportive reminder of the steps to making a collage. Our next step was to seek an artist whose work would inspire children to investigate ways of using the more complex material in their collages. We highlighted *My Dog Is as Smelly as Dirty Socks* by Hanoch Piven and drew special attention to the fabric details he used, such as the sock representing the dog's ears.

MAIN MATERIAL

We offered felt in a wide range of colors as the main material. Felt is a great foundation for collage, as its texture prevents loose parts from slipping out of place.

Typically the base (called the *support* by collagists) is the first thing students choose in the collage makerspace. We have used

- felt squares,
- placemats,
- enlarged photographs,

Parker, age six, selects a support that matches her idea and arranges the loose parts to match her sketch.

- decorative calendar pages,
- scrapbook paper,
- pieces of fabric,
- canvases, and
- metal trays.

LOOSE PARTS

After the children have selected the material for their base, or support, they choose loose parts to make their collages. In the collage makerspace, children use loose parts to learn about and become fluent with creating collages that include texture, balance, contrast, movement, proportion, pattern, variety, and unity (Brommer 1994). For this makerspace the loose parts included, among other things,

- fabric strips,
- string,
- wool,
- yarn,

- ribbon,
- shoelaces,
- rickrack,
- embroidery thread,
- fabric-covered buttons,
- yarn,
- lace, and
- tulle.

Many easily available loose parts work well in collages. If you have access to the outdoors, loose parts from nature can be gathered by a class or small group of children. We have taken students on nature walks and gathered mulch, pine needles, acorns, twigs, seed pods, leaves, moss, and more.

Loose parts in the collage makerspace with textile loose parts

Adaptation for the Youngest Makers

To scaffold young children in exploring how loose parts can represent features of a character or idea they imagine, provide pictures and faces along with loose parts so they can place parts on top of the images and make this connection.

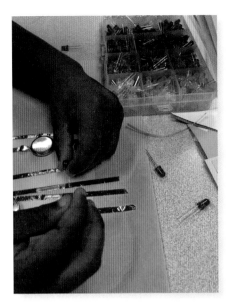

Marlie tries to connect the circuit.

Marlie continues to practice connecting circuits, figuring out the easiest and most efficient way to do so.

Marlie succeeds after persevering through many attempts!

Marlie persevered and successfully connected the circuits in her collage.

She wanted to light the candles on the birthday cake. She could hardly wait to figure out how to connect the paper circuits and light her candles.

When she figured out how to connect the circuit, Marlie excitedly decided to add more details and more circuits. She added a house but couldn't think of where to put a light in it. As she was contemplating, she came up with a new and wonderful idea. She would make a dragon and have "fire" (a paper circuit) come out of its foot!

And that's exactly what she did!

As a more knowledgeable peer, she then helped others figure out how to connect the copper foil, battery, and LED lights. When she was finished, she shared her project with the others at her makerspace and used her maker talk as an opportunity to talk about some of the difficulties she encountered while trying to get her circuit to work. Her maker talk inspired the others to persevere and continue working toward creating beautiful and meaningful collages that included circuitry.

Marlie enacted the learning practices of the maker movement as she created her lighted collage. Below is a sample of our observations.

Documenting Learning in the Collage Makerspace

Learning Practices that Lead to the Development of a Maker Mindset	Indicators of Learning through Enactment of the Practices
Inquire	• Marlie was excited to figure out how to make the circuit light. She asked lots of questions.
Tinker	• Marlie had to play and tinker before she got an idea to make a birthday cake. She cut the pieces of paper and arranged and rearranged them.
Seek and Share Resources	• Marlie shared her difficulties in a maker talk and helped others avoid the same mistakes.
Hack and Repurpose	• When Marlie couldn't figure out how to use a light in the house in her next collage, she hacked and repurposed her collage to include a dragon instead, to fit her thinking and making.
Express Intent	• Marlie expressed her desire to figure out how to make a paper circuit light up.
Develop Fluency	• Marlie had previously practiced collage with paper and developed fluency with its uses. She could now focus her efforts toward learning the workings, connections, and setup of paper circuits.
Simplify to Complexify	• Marlie used simple materials (paper, copper foil, LED light, and a battery) to create a complex story that included a birthday cake and a dragon. Marlie built self-efficacy, confidence, and agency as she figured out how to make a circuit while simultaneously creating a meaningful collage.

Paper circuits are a complex tool in collage, as indicated in the developmental continuum. You have many other, simpler options for materials, tools, and attachments in this makerspace. Below are examples of collage makerspaces we set up in formal and informal learning environments, using a variety of materials. We hope they inspire you as you create a collage makerspace for your children.

More Collage Makerspaces to Inspire Your Making

The following photos show just some of our many variations on the collage makerspace. If you don't have the exact resources pictured, don't let it delay you. You can create an engaging makerspace with almost any materials you already have on hand.

Metal base with metal loose parts

Jansen, age six, making a robot collage

Paper base with natural loose parts

Natural loose parts in collage makerspace

Felt base with glass loose parts

Children playing and making with glass loose parts in collage makerspace

Contact paper base with plastic loose parts

Children playing and making with plastic loose parts in collage makerspace

Paper base with paper loose parts

Children playing and making with paper loose parts in collage makerspace

Making a Mark by making gifts for others to express emotion and demonstrate gratitude. Hayley decided to make this collage for her mom. Mother's Day was coming up, and she thought her mother would love the natural parts of it because her mom "loves acorns and nature."

Sharing Our Thinking

Children are naturally drawn to collage because it highlights common materials used in new ways or introduces new loose parts and found materials. The following lesson can be used when introducing a new material or new way of making collages in the collage makerspace.

COLLAGE MAKERSPACE FOCUS LESSON

Objective: Children will imagine new ways to play with textures by using plastic materials to make collages.

MATERIALS

- maker collage anchor chart
- clear contact paper
- transparent plastic pieces (We cut up old plastic folders, but you could also use cellophane or acetate.)
- containers with lids to hold the plastic pieces
- camera for documentation
- tape (We taped the contact paper to the table so it didn't move while the children were sticking and unsticking.)
- light table (If you don't have one, an overhead projector or natural light works well too!)

Focus and Explore

Connect: *"We have been learning about how the light can pass through some materials, while it will not pass through other materials. While I was thinking about it, I had a great idea! We could select a collage base that light could pass through! I wonder, what will our collages look like if our materials are all transparent or translucent? So today we will imagine new ways to play with textures using plastic materials to make collages."*

Teach: Hold up some translucent loose parts to the light or place them on the light table. *"See how the light passes through these loose parts?"* Hold the contact paper up to the light. *"What do you notice about this new material?"* They may say it's sticky on one side or note that the light passes through it, even more than it does the translucent materials. Model how to be sure the sticky side is up and how to stick the plastic pieces to the contact paper. Act as though you want to change your mind: *"Wait a minute. I want to move this piece."* Model how to peel it off the contact paper and rearrange it.

Active Involvement: Pass around the piece of contact paper with several loose parts stuck to it. Let the children feel the texture and try taking off the loose parts and sticking them back onto the contact paper.

Imagine

Use the translucent loose parts as inspiration. Ask, *"What could you make with these translucent shapes of plastic?"* Record their ideas on the Class at a Glance form (see appendix C).

Play and Make

Give the children plenty of time to experiment, play, and make with the new materials. They will want to peel and unpeel the pieces to represent their changing thinking and test the affordances of the materials as they enact tinkering, hacking, and repurposing. Observe the children and select a couple of different ideas, collages, or stories to highlight during the "Share" segment. Notice if they use one another as resources for how-to questions or to solve a problem. Young children seek resources to help them solve problems. Document their collages by taking photos and using the Learning Practices Documentation form (see appendix B).

Share

Share and celebrate the unique collages made by the students, all using the same materials.

Select a child for the maker talk who experienced difficulties or may have needed advice from peers. Have the child identify the problem they encountered and then give them an opportunity to seek advice from other makers.

SUGGESTED BOOKS TO INSPIRE MAKERS WITH COLLAGE

In the collage makerspace, we recommend children's books that use collage in the illustrations. This list of recommended titles includes books that show a variety of materials used in collages to inspire young learners:

Snippets: A Story about Paper Shapes by Diane Alber
Dragons, Wagons, Wings & Swings by Rancier Alongi
Leaf Man by Lois Ehlert
The Scraps Book by Lois Ehlert
Matisse's Garden by Samantha Friedman
Faces by Zoe Miller and David Goodman
My Dog Is as Smelly as Dirty Socks by Hanoch Piven
The Perfect Purple Feather by Hanoch Piven
Faces by François Robert and Jean Robert
Blackout by John Rocco (for paper circuits)

Next Steps in Your Transformation

By creating an intentional makerspace and providing time for playing and making with collage materials, you are providing opportunities for young collagists to enact the learning practices of the maker movement and build a maker mindset. As you introduce materials for the base (felt, photos, placemats, construction paper) and loose parts (shells, twigs, bottle caps), children quickly learn to layer loose parts to represent their complex thinking and meanings. After documenting their enactment of the learning practices, take a moment to think about their development of a maker mindset. For example, have you noticed your children's excitement about new loose parts in the collage makerspace? This shows their growing sense of wonder. Have you documented the many ways children tinker with, study, and test materials and use them to represent many different things in their collages? This is all evidence that children are becoming mindful observers. At this point you may want to have a maker talk with your colleagues to share, collaborate, and consider next steps in the transformation of your collage makerspaces.

- What loose parts do your children seem most drawn to? Can you get the children to use them differently to build other aspects of the maker mindsets?
- If you don't have room to create a new makerspace, how can you make your collage makerspace portable and usable at an individual student's desk or table?
- What learning practices have you observed in children as they play and make in the collage makerspace? How are these behaviors connected to the maker mindset?
- Ask your children, "What have you learned about becoming a maker? What new skills do you have as a collagist?" Reflect on how their answers are connected to the maker mindset.

WHAT CAN YOU IMAGINE

— MAKING —

WITH THESE CONSTRUCTION MATERIALS?

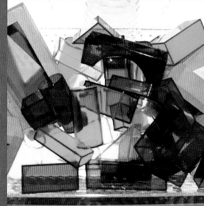

An invitation for children to imagine, play, and make
with construction materials

CHAPTER 4

Construction Makerspaces

CONSTRUCTION

Now touching my blocks, fingers eager to make.
Stacking, crashing, falling; sometimes I frustrate.
Shiny glass gems draw my courage back in.
Tinkering and remaking, I'm confident again.
New ideas spark as I repurpose these things.
Glass beads with blocks become the jewels of kings.

Stories to Inspire Making

As the children approached the construction makerspace one morning, they gathered around a basket of architectural blocks with arches, planks, textured triangles, and cubes stained with shapes that evoked memories of windows. As they entered the makerspace, they noticed new materials: mirror shapes, frosted green glass gems, and iridescent mosaic tiles reminiscent of stained glass windows glimmering in clear containers. The children instantly poured the containers out onto the carpet with awe and excitement, selecting and closely examining each new piece. As they touched each new object, they commented on how it felt smooth and hard.

An invitation for children to play and make with wood blocks and glass loose parts

They were curious about how the glass materials sounded when they clinked together. Since all materials have the ability to open new learning pathways in young children (Pacini-Ketchabaw, Kind, and Kocher 2016; Taguchi 2011), the children entered a rich world of experiences as they were inspired by the materials and began to imagine, play, and make structures from their imaginations.

Cole, age four, was stacking the blocks to explore how tall he could build his imagined structure. "What are these?" he asked with wide eyes when he noticed the new loose parts. He began exploring the textures, colors, and shapes of the materials and was curious how he could use them in his building. He spread the playdough attachment onto the blocks to secure his chosen treasures as his construction grew. "This is my jewelry collection," he proudly announced as he continued to make. The materials helped him imagine a way to make something that developed his sense of wonder.

We took his lead and brought in inspiration for his investigation of the properties and types of jewelry. Over the next week, images of jewelry, rock and mineral books, and actual stones were incorporated into the makerspace to spark more creative thinking and making as the children developed their relationships with the materials. On this shared journey, the children learned more about a topic and constructed their ideas and stories by playing and making in this construction makerspace.

The children explore the new materials by stacking and tinkering with what the attachments can do.

The construction makerspace is repurposed with inspiring projections, books about rocks and minerals, and new gem loose parts to reflect the children's interests.

Why Is Construction the Next Makerspace to Introduce to Children?

Open-ended questions and loose parts in a construction makerspace

The children had been learning to express their thoughts, feelings, and intentions using the three-dimensional medium of collage and other aesthetic techniques in their making experiences. Construction, a more complex three-dimensional technique, enlarges a child's concepts of form and space relationships. "Construction offers a special opportunity for invention because a variety of materials can be put together in many ways to create new forms" (Lord 1958, 5). When children make with blocks and other construction materials, they are physically and literally building, making, and communicating stories or information they know. In her 2017 book, *Creative Block Play*, Roseanne Regan Hansel emphasizes that "all young children bring a great deal of knowledge and experience about their world, which they are able to eagerly express through their block building" (10). Block play not only elicits frequent and high-quality oral language but also allows children to use a block to represent something they imagine making. This type of symbolic representation is a foundation for learning to read and write symbols.

Remaking a Block Area into a Construction Makerspace

When we first observed children and their thinking processes in building with blocks throughout a variety of pre-K classrooms, we focused on the main material provided in the space. We provided experiences for children to build with different and increasingly complex types of blocks to create a continuum of block materials to be introduced throughout the year in parallel with planned STEAM studies. For example, we offered nature or wooden blocks at the beginning of the year when the children were studying nature and their new school community. Later in the year, we introduced larger-scale materials, including cardboard boxes, that required a higher level of complexity in attachments as the children studied buildings and structures. New materials kept the block center interesting. However, we felt the children needed further opportunities to engage in the learning practices of the maker movement. Our first wave of transformation was to include loose parts, which increased the children's tinkering, hacking, and repurposing behavior as they evaluated the properties of new materials and used and reused them to represent a part of their structure or story. The list below offers ideas for transforming your block area or STEAM building space into a construction makerspace with materials you may already have.

Designing Your First Construction Makerspace

Inspiration and Support	• Children's book(s) showing a character tinkering and building with materials (*Rex Wrecks It!* or *Dreaming Up*); read and set out copies as inspiration • Makerspace sign to encourage making ("What can you imagine making with these building materials?") • Focus lesson demonstrating how to play and make with wooden blocks
Main Materials	• Start with what you have! Cardboard blocks or wooden unit blocks are in most early learning classrooms and are a great first material to encourage open-ended play and making at the beginning of the year.
Loose Parts	• Choose any category of loose parts, or look around the room for what you have. Collect sticks and rocks outside for a free and engaging way to add complexity into children's designs.
Tools and Attachments	• Not necessary at the beginning. If children become frustrated with their block structures falling, you may incorporate playdough to add stability to their designs.

Before and after of the transformation from block area to emerging construction makerspace

Another important characteristic of the maker movement is the use of authentic materials and tools. When our block centers transformed into construction makerspaces, we included wooden blocks and scraps and real tools, such as hammers, sandpaper, screwdrivers, and screws, to allow children to develop a fluency and competence with diverse tools. With this addition we expanded our definition of a construction makerspace beyond the power of blocks alone.

Our construction makerspaces have included blocks, Legos, cardboard, woodworking, robotic blocks, and solid materials for three-dimensional constructions that represent the creative imagination of the child. We included attachments at times so children could investigate the engineering concepts of stability and balance, and simplify to complexify by combining and connecting materials to make new meaning. Some blocks, such as Legos, Bristle Blocks, and Magna-Tiles, have built-in attachments. However, when working with unit blocks, foam blocks, or even structural planks, it might be helpful to include playdough or hook-and-loop attachments so children can demonstrate their ability to explore new ways to connect and build their structures, settings, and three-dimensional creations.

Marina Umaschi Bers (2008) notes, "There is a continuum of learning opportunities that extends from blocks to robots" (14). As you move across the continuum from the arts-and-crafts materials of blocks, wooden discs, and Legos to the high-tech realm of electronic gadgets, magnetic tiles, electric tools, and more, children always love to play with blocks. The progression of construction from stacking to building enclosures is also observed in these makerspaces. After your children

Adaptations for the Youngest Makers

Toddlers may be at the stage of moving, touching, holding, or dumping the blocks, with little or no building. Begin by modeling how to stack the blocks vertically or lay them out horizontally to support children's growing understanding of how to play and make with blocks.

have spent several weeks playing and making with the main material of a type of block you selected, we recommend changing the main material to increase their fluency. Use the continuum below to select the next main material to sustain your construction makerspace throughout the year.

Maker's Continuum of Playing and Making for Construction

Arts and Crafts			High Tech
Children select a main material with which to build, stack, and construct their imaginings: • unit blocks • cardboard blocks • Bristle Blocks • Duplo or Lego bricks • structural planks • magnetic tiles They incorporate loose parts to represent their thinking throughout their designs.	Children use more complex tools and attachment techniques with cardboard to construct their designs: • cardboard scissors, saws • hot glue or cardboard attachment techniques	Children use authentic woodworking tools and materials to construct their designs: • wood scraps • hammers • screwdrivers • hand drills • sandpaper • handsaws • nails, screws	Children connect robotic blocks to build and program structures to perform specific tasks: • Cubelets • littleBits

STREAM Learning in the Construction Makerspace

The power of block and construction materials to strengthen the understanding of STREAM subjects is highly documented. "Children who are exploring building materials will also become meaningfully involved in mathematics as they build with blocks and other materials" (Chalufour and Worth 2004, 7). However, as we observed countless children playing and making with construction materials, we identified behaviors that align with other content areas. The prompts below will help you ensure that your children make these interdisciplinary connections as well.

Prompts to Ensure STREAM Learning Connections

Science

Makers will do the following:

- Develop models of familiar or imagined structures or settings using construction materials ("What structures/places/settings can you imagine making with these construction materials?")
- Compare the effects of stacking different materials to achieve heights and lengths and to make stable structures ("How can you build with these materials to make a stable structure?")

Technology

- Use appropriate tools (hammers, screwdrivers) to attach materials and make three-dimensional models ("What is the best tool to use to construct your model?")
- Code or stack programmable blocks to make robots follow the desired actions ("What code or actions can you imagine programming with these blocks?")

Reading/Literacy

- Use three-dimensional constructions and models to communicate their ideas with others ("What information can you share to teach others about your construction?")
- Use construction materials to build, share, and illustrate settings for their stories ("What details can you add to your settings to tell your readers more about the place you are building?")

Engineering

- Develop a simple sketch to illustrate use of construction materials ("What can you sketch to plan out your design with these construction materials?")
- Identify problems and develop improved structures while making ("How can you make your structures stable using all these materials? How can you improve your design?")
- Imagine, play, make, remake, and share using the construction materials ("Where are you in the Maker Cycle, and what are your next steps?")

Arts

- Grow as artists by considering the elements of design in their constructions ("How can you include symmetry/balance in your design as you play and make?")

Mathematics

- Make structures with geometric shapes ("What can you imagine making with theses shapes?")
- Notice and tinker with how many blocks it takes to achieve a certain length ("How long/high can you make your structure using these construction materials?")
- Experience symmetry in design and become aware of balance and the patterns needed to make their structures stable ("What patterns do you notice in your structure/construction?")

Imagine Making a Construction Makerspace

The purpose of this construction makerspace was to develop the identity of the builder by increasing tinkering behaviors with the addition of loose parts to the building materials. The children had been investigating the properties of reflective materials throughout their day, and adding metal loose parts in the construction makerspace encouraged the children to continue their in-depth investigations in an open-ended way.

A construction makerspace to build and make with metal materials: 1. Inspiration and support (book and sign) 2. Main material (wood blocks) 3. Loose parts (foil and metal pieces) 4. Tools and attachments (hot glue gun, woodworking tools nearby)

The Most Magnificent Thing by Ashley Spires invited and inspired the children to work with metal. The class had read this book earlier in the year to understand how makers think and act when making. Now we highlighted the images of the girl putting together metallic pieces to make three-dimensional constructions. The phrases "she smooths," "the girl tinkers and hammers and measures," and "she twists and tweaks and fastens" modeled how the children could manipulate the materials to achieve the visions they imagined. The guiding question for this investigation was "What can you build and make with these metal materials?"

MAIN MATERIAL

The main material selected for this makerspace was wood scraps that children could cover with foil or stack together to make the shapes they imagined. The continuum of construction materials above shows how children can work up to levels of complexity of materials and tools as they learn to use them properly and safely to build with confidence. Froebel's uses of open-ended "toys" are evident in the ways children imagine, play, make, and share block re-creations of their worlds (Lange 2018).

Hansel (2017) provides a nice overview of other block building materials in the following categories:

- cardboard blocks and large hollow blocks (great for making child-size structures)
- nature blocks and wood scraps
- foam blocks
- designer blocks (hardwood blocks in a variety of colors and three-dimensional shapes, such as Grimm's blocks)
- structural planks (Kapla, Keva, and Dr. Drew's Discovery Blocks can be used on tabletops or the floor; they foster investigations of balance and stability and require only simple stacking.)
- connection blocks (Legos, Duplos, and Bristle Blocks offer interlocking construction materials and translucent magnetic blocks that stay in place.)
- tabletop blocks (architectural unit blocks, wood scraps, and translucent blocks and shapes that can be used on a light table)
- robotic blocks (Programmable blocks, such as Cubelets, prompt the maker to identify a goal and then follow a "robot recipe" to make the pieces function correctly. For example, you always need to include a "sense" Cubelet to take in information, a "think" Cubelet to send the signals in the right direction, and an "act" Cubelet to initiate an action, such as spinning, making sounds, or lighting up.)

Adaptations for Makers with Special Rights

For children with physical disabilities, Hansel (2017) recommends foam blocks because they are lightweight and easy to grip.

This child selects a wood piece and covers it with loose-part pieces of foil to begin his construction.

LOOSE PARTS

To increase tinkering behaviors in representing the stories and ideas the children were imagining, we selected metal loose parts. The character in our inspirational book was tinkering with metal bits and pieces, and also, metal is harder to manipulate and change in shape, which prompted the children to evaluate properties and test their designs when adding loose parts to their constructions. "Building and constructing with loose parts allows children to translate abstract images in their mind and creatively turn these images into concrete objects" (Daly and Beloglovsky 2015, 162). In this example, metal loose parts included

- mirror tiles,
- screws,
- washers,
- binder clips,
- metal thread spools,
- paper clips, and
- foil.

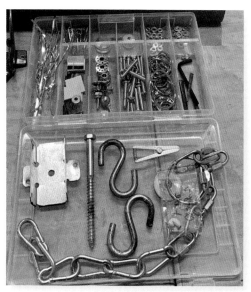

Close-up of metal loose parts

TOOLS AND ATTACHMENTS

Certain construction materials require specific tools to make and connect pieces together. For example, cardboard requires more complex tools to cut and change shapes. Therefore, the tools in this makerspace included the following:

- cardboard scissors (Canary products recommended)
- cardboard saws

Recommended woodworking tools (especially products by www.forsmallhands .com) include the following:

- handsaw sets
- safety glasses
- stubby screwdriver
- hand drill
- clamp-on vise

In this makerspace children had access to nails, hammers, and saws in a nearby woodworking makerspace at The Muse Knoxville children's museum.

Safety reminders on using authentic tools in the Make Space at The Muse Knoxville, a children's museum

Learning specific attachment techniques for cardboard gives learners opportunities to grow their builder identities. For the first attachment lessons, all you need is tape! Then you can increase children's fluency with attachments such as

- brass fasteners,
- string,
- hot glue, and
- wire.

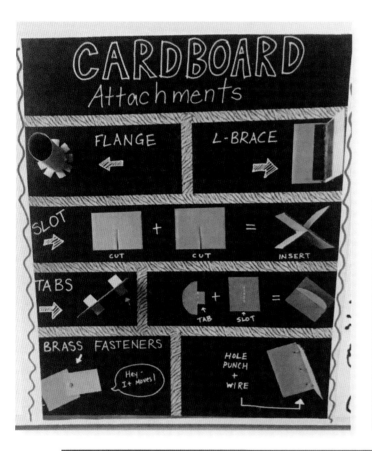

The continuum of attachment techniques displayed at The Muse Knoxville, from cardboard attachments to Cubelets

Children learn how to attach blocks to make what they imagine and then practice more complex attachment techniques, building a strong foundation for programming the robots they imagine. With that in mind, let's talk about the powerful learning that takes place when children imagine, play, make, and share in construction makerspaces.

Spaces for Playing and Making

The children, ages two to four, were invited to play and make one morning in a new construction makerspace in a home learning area. The intention was to develop their identities as builders and storytellers as they inquired about the new plastic materials and loose parts and imagined and made structures and stories. Our inspirational book, *Be a Maker* by Katey Howes, showed a child waking up and imagining all the possibilities for making, just as our children were doing. The main material was translucent tabletop blocks, and the loose parts were plastic cups of

Construction makerspace with tabletop translucent blocks and plastic loose parts

different colors, shapes, and sizes, plus cellophane pieces and rolls. The only tool was scissors, but one child added tape in his engineering process.

Cole, age four, went straight to the cellophane and said, "Oh, this looks creative!" He displayed evidence of learning by inquiring about the material's properties, folding, molding, and finally cutting pieces of the cellophane to see what would happen. When he placed the new material on the table, it formed a cone-like shape and he said, "I just built a mountaintop!"

Cole imagines making a mountaintop with the cellophane.

The mountaintop transforms into a princess hat.

Cole then noticed the plastic cups. He began stacking the cups and stuffing the cellophane inside, tinkering and testing out the properties of these materials to once again imagine making something different, a princess hat. A few minutes later, he relocated the cups and cellophane rolls to a larger building surface, the floor.

Imagining a trap to make with lots and lots of tape

Cole imagined a new idea every few minutes with the change of the material. He then expressed his intention to build a trap. Huge pieces of cellophane covered the floor, and he repurposed the princess hat again as a volcano. Then he discovered the tape in the closet and asked me for it. When asked why he needed the tape, he said, "I just need the tape for my art!" Well, how can you argue with that? As he manipulated the tape, gaining fluency with its possibilities, he narrated that the lines he was making with it looked like a roller coaster. After his large-scale investigation of how to make a trap on the floor, Cole began collecting the resources to make his trap on the light table.

Making his dinosaur trap and sharing how it works with others

This time he used the tape intentionally to attach his dinosaur's head to its body so it remained secure as he played and shared his story. "It's called the dinosaur trap! Looks pretty scary, doesn't it?" Cole explained how his trap worked in his maker talk. He explained that the people come to this land because it is so beautiful. They try to get the jewels that are around the volcanoes, but just as they try to take one, a dinosaur jumps out and traps them. The dinosaurs make the people bring them food, and they live the rest of their lives in the dinosaur world.

Organization/Aesthetics

Consider adding a dedicated space in your construction makerspace for structures that are still in process. Provide "Making in Progress" signs to remind others to respect children's work.

Documenting Learning in the Construction Makerspace

Learning Practices that Lead to the Development of a Maker Mindset	Indicators of Learning through Enactment of the Practices
Inquire	• Cole investigated materials and questioned what he could make.
Tinker	• Cole stacked, built, crumpled, and stuffed cellophane to determine form and function.
Seek and Share Resources	• Cole used materials' form and function to make hypotheses about what he could do with them.
Hack and Repurpose	• Cole repurposed the materials from his princess hat, making them into a volcano.
Express Intent	• Cole stated he was going to build a trap.
Develop Fluency	• Cole practiced using tape and improved.
Simplify to Complexify	• Cole used simple materials to make a story that reflected his complex thinking.

More Construction Makerspaces to Inspire Your Making

Here are more construction makerspaces to inspire you as you imagine places where children can build with a variety of materials. These examples follow the continuum as, over the course of the year, children study the specific properties of materials.

Wood blocks with natural loose parts

Architectural blocks with glass loose parts

Structural planks with glass loose parts

Duplos with wood loose parts that were inspired by the photo of the structure

Legos with plastic loose parts that could be explored to add movement to their creations

Cardboard with paper loose parts

Woodworking with wood scraps and metal loose parts

Cubelets robotic blocks with support cards
describing the function of each block

CHAPTER 5

Sculpture Makerspaces

My hands use clay to squish, pinch, and mold.
Ideas take shape and creatures unfold.
Creations of robots, pirates, and ships—
Lumps of clay become whimsical trips.

Stories to Inspire Making

Children of all ages were invited to explore and tinker with playdough set out on oven trays on the four tables in the pop-up makerspace. The large trays welcomed children to coil, pinch, roll, and set their imaginations free on this main material. Children sculpted individually in some areas and created in small groups in others. Specks of iridescence shimmering in the gray playdough contrasted with the darkness of the black playdough. Subtle metallic shades of silver and gold glowed from metal loose parts organized in muffin tins.

An invitation for children to make in a playdough makerspace with metal loose parts

The children and the materials were about to embark together on a journey of making. Sylvia Kind (2014) describes how artists and makers follow materials as they work with them. Children join *with* the materials as they squish, mold, and shape the material. Although every child from ages two to ten had access to the same materials, they all joined in the process of making with the material, asking, "What can the playdough do?" and "What can I imagine this playdough becoming?" Bill, a seven-year-old in second grade, said that he knew a lot about the Great Wall of China. The gray playdough had pulled at this knowledge inside his head, and he sculpted the wall with the lines and spaces he remembered seeing in images. He explained what he wanted others to know when viewing his piece: "It took over two hundred years to build. The king of China started, and then he had a son that continued the project."

Bill, a second grader, shares his knowledge about the Great Wall of China as he makes.

As more children began playing, curious about the new materials in the sculpture makerspace, three-dimensional representations of their imaginings formed right in front of our eyes: A shooting-star robot with a metal bit carefully placed to make the engine. An iPad, with an accurate number of buttons, that the maker encountered in her daily life. Even a pirate character, complete with treasure map and a chest of metallic treasures. Each sculpture had a purpose (what the child wanted to communicate), each held significant meaning for the child, and each embodied a piece of the child's creativity and imagination for others to enjoy.

Charlie, age four, explains how the metallic parts in her sculpture make her shooting star fly.

Eleanor, age five, explains how to use her iPad.

Sumaya, age seven, sculpted a story of a pirate adventure.

Why Is Sculpture the Next Makerspace to Introduce to Children?

After making three-dimensional art with collage and experiencing whole-body play with construction materials, children explore shaping and forming their constructions to make a sculpture. Traditional sculpture is carved or modeled out of materials (Lord 1958). Children easily connect to sculpture because it relates to previous tactile experiences of making and creates an instant relationship with playdough, clay, and other mediums. As they move on to sculpture, our young makers can connect to their prior experiences of hands-on making and add depth to their understanding of what it means to be a sculptor, how the materials work, and how they can shape a moldable material to represent ideas by moving it up, pushing it down, and stretching it out (Pelo 2007).

Remaking a Playdough Area into a Sculpture Makerspace

When we first started working with preschool teachers, playdough was often the only sculpting material offered to children. We observed its benefits, such as improving dexterity as children manipulated the clay (squishing, squeezing, pulling, and pushing), but we wanted to increase the complexity of play in order to observe the learning practices in action and increase children's knowledge of what it means to be a maker. At higher grade levels, children only used sculptural mediums in art class or as an end-of-unit project to show what they had learned over a course of study. Community art classes provided children with clay or other sculptural materials but with the goal of making an end product that was the same for all. Standards or learning goals were always represented, of course, and children still had many opportunities to explore and develop curiosity, fine-motor skills, and social skills as they played alongside each other.

Still, these centers and community activities lacked the loose parts, variety of materials, and intentional planning for the bigger purpose of developing a maker mindset that are key to makerspaces. We wanted to ask questions that supported children's imaginings and give them opportunities to tinker as they made something important to them. So we began the transformation from playdough area to sculpture makerspace using the main material that nearly everyone already had on hand: playdough! Use the makerspace design below as inspiration to begin your own transformation.

Adaptations for the Youngest Makers

Provide plenty of time for toddlers and preschoolers to explore the playdough and clay materials with their whole bodies. Encourage them to dig into the clay with their toes and fingers. Then begin modeling how to push and pull the clay to create new shapes and textures.

Designing Your First Sculpture Makerspace

Inspiration and Support

- Clay poem from VanDerwater's *With My Hands* to inspire children in making shapes, or another children's book or poem featuring clay in illustrations
- Makerspace sign to encourage making ("What can you imagine making with these sculpting materials?")
- Focus lesson demonstrating how to roll and make simple shapes with playdough

Main Material

- Start with what you already have access to if possible. You can buy the cheapest sculpting material, playdough, or make your own at home. Limit colors to one or two choices so children focus on what they can shape instead of mixing colors.

Loose Parts

- Gather one or two types of grass or flowers from around your area to add color to the designs. Nature materials allow children to easily change the shape of or add to their sculpture by breaking and tearing off the pieces they need.

Tools and Attachments

- Simple rollers or shape cutters are a good place to start. Remove the predetermined cookie-cutter characters and shapes from your tools and encourage children to imagine their own things to make with open-ended shapes (circles, squares, triangles).

Before and after of the transformation from playdough area to emerging sculpture makerspace

Our next goal in this makerspace was to give children access to a greater variety of sculpture materials throughout the year and teach them how to make with more complex materials and tools. The continuum of materials used in this makerspace begins with playdough and proceeds through making with many sorts of clay, found materials, and foil, all the way to different gauges of wire, including pipe cleaners, floral wire, and coated wire. This makerspace includes tools and attachments for carving, imprinting, and cutting playdough. Parts of this continuum can be found in Ann Pelo's beautiful book *The Language of Art* (2007), in which she begins with clay. Use the continuum below to select the next main materials and tools to sustain your makerspace over time.

Maker's Continuum of Playing and Making for Sculpture

Arts and Crafts

High Tech

Children explore the properties of the main material, squishing, rolling, pinching, and sculpting their imaginings and incorporating loose parts to represent their thinking: • playdough • modeling clay • natural clay	Children generalize what they have learned about attachment techniques and tools and select the most efficient method as they work with found or recyclable materials and incorporate loose parts into their sculptures: • cardboard and paper • plastic • foil	Children explore new attachment techniques and refine their sculpting abilities with the more resistant materials and incorporate more complex loose parts in sculptures: • wire • old machines for taking apart and repurposing objects into their designs	Children create features or add movement to sculptures using circuits and other high-tech sculpting materials and tools: • conductive dough • LEDs • buzzers • fans

STREAM Learning in the Sculpture Makerspace

When children sculpt they engage in interdisciplinary learning in the roles of scientist, engineer, mathematician, and artist and use literacy skills to represent their ideas when communicating what they made by speaking or writing. Use the prompts below as you observe children making in the sculpture makerspace to ensure connections across disciplines and meet content area standards.

Prompts to Ensure STREAM Learning Connections

Science	Makers will do the following: • Question properties of a material and how it can change when molded with their hands ("What do you notice about this sculpting material? How can you change the shape to match what you imagine making?")
Technology	• Use authentic tools to add detail or designs to the sculpture ("What details or marks can you make in the sculpture to bring life to your design?")
Reading/Literacy	• Imagine information or stories that the material evokes and share them orally or in writing. ("What stories do you imagine as you make with this sculpting material?" or "What information can you teach others about the object you have sculpted?")
Engineering	• Discover ways to attach pieces of clay ("How can you attach the pieces of your clay together? Try it and evaluate how well it works.")
Arts	• Incorporate shapes into the sculpture by tinkering and testing how pieces fit together and overlap. How can you add pieces to your sculpture so it is shaped like you imagine?
Mathematics	• Use tools to measure and weigh the amounts and lengths they imagine needing in their sculpture ("How much clay do you need for your making?") • Investigate patterns that add to the texture and style of their piece ("What patterns do you notice in your design?")

Imagine Making a Sculpture Makerspace

The purpose of this makerspace was to develop the children's identities as sculptors and artists while increasing their fluency with tools. These children had many previous experiences with playing and making with playdough, so we invited them to express their imaginings with modeling clay. New sculpting tools allowed them to incorporate texture into their design and tinker with making bumpy, rough, and smooth surfaces.

Clay makerspace with nature loose parts:
1. Inspiration and support (book and sign) 2. Main material (modeling clay) 3. Loose parts (sticks, pine cones, birdseed) 4. Tools and attachments (wooden rollers and clay-sculpting tools)

INSPIRATION AND SUPPORT

The children had been making and sharing stories with playdough, and we now wanted them to explore a material that had more substance but was still malleable to their budding sculpting skills. Before setting up this sculpture makerspace, we discovered books that would inspire the children in working with the new main material. We selected *Claymates* by Dev Petty, in which artist Lauren Eldridge used polymer clay to illustrate the brown and gray shapes that make up the characters. Children wonder what will happen as the clay balls become characters in the artist's hands and then begin to shape themselves. Because of its strong models of authentic tools in use, we knew this book had to be the inspiration and support in our new sculpture makerspace. We added a guiding question to help provoke children's imaginations: "What can you imagine making with clay?"

MAIN MATERIALS

In this makerspace we moved into air-dry clay mediums. Pelo (2017) divides sculptural materials into three categories: clay, found materials, and wire. She recommends introducing them to children in that order, over time, because the skill level needed to work with these materials increases. Clay types range from manufactured modeling clays to earthen clays and can be found at your local craft stores. Here are some recommended main materials for your sculpture makerspaces:

- Playdough is suggested first because it is affordable and accessible to many educators and caregivers. It is easily made at home or purchased at local stores. Playdough is easy to press, bend, squeeze, twist, and tear, allowing children to tinker, take risks with new sculptural techniques, and build confidence in their abilities before moving on to denser materials like clay or resistant materials like wire.
- Modeling and polymer clays, as shown in the highlighted makerspace, are a great next step. Modeling clay is an oil-based material and is introduced next because it remains malleable and can be used over and over again without drying out. This is a favorite material for animators because it is reusable. Polymer is a plastic-based clay but hardens when baked in an oven. According to Taylor (2014), this is the perfect material for young sculptors because it is soft and the shape can be easily changed when the clay is conditioned.

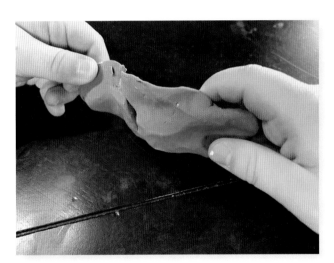

A child begins to explore the modeling clay to discover how it can change.

Organization/ Aesthetics

When working with clay, protect your work surface. Wax paper, roll paper, plastic tablecloths, newspaper, drop cloths, and cardboard are all good materials to shield your work surface from stains and sticky residue.

Adaptations for Makers with Special Rights

For children who experience tactile sensory aversions to playdough or clay, try placing the material in a sealed clear plastic bag. This may make it easier for children to touch the clay and increase their tolerance of the texture as they inquire and tinker. For children who may mouth objects when playing, use playdough made from natural ingredients and observe their play carefully. If you choose to scent the dough, do so only when children are ready for this added exposure, and use only pure, food-grade essential oils or herbs.

- Air-dry clays are relatively inexpensive and don't require heating to harden. They do require specific techniques for joining pieces, and water is needed as you work with this material. Once the clay dries, it cannot be reshaped again. We have used air-dry clay in pop-up makerspaces for organizations that do not have access to or funding for kiln firing.
- Found materials, such as cardboard boxes and plastic bottles, are described by Pelo (2007) as "disposable materials" that "offer intriguing provocation" for sculpture (74).
- Foil is harder to manipulate and shape and requires more complex attachment techniques to hold pieces together.
- Wire is a hard and resistant material that requires willpower and strong hand muscles to shape.

LOOSE PARTS

Loose parts are an excellent way to incorporate texture in sculpture. "Texture is the tactile quality of the surface of an object or a work of art" (Daly and Beloglovsky 2015, 38). With each touch these materials spark a desire to tinker, explore, and describe ("Is it prickly, soft, rough, silky?").

In this makerspace nature loose parts invited children to explore different textures. The following materials made their way into the stories and explanations of what the children made:

- birdseed
- pine cones
- sticks

TOOLS AND ATTACHMENTS

Sculpture incorporates a wide variety of tools because the main materials encompass so many different mediums. When using playdough and clay, anything can be a clay tool. One of our favorite new tools comes from Cassie Stephens, author of *Clay Lab for Kids* (2017), who explains that gently scrubbing the surface of the clay with a dampened toothbrush accomplishes the slip-and-score attachment method. Lace, burlap, textured plastic and packing bubbles, cardboard, and even the soles of shoes can be used to stamp texture into the medium. Another fascinating technique is using loose parts to add texture, thus transforming them into tools.

For this makerspace we purchased wood-handled, double-ended clay-sculpting tools for cutting, carving, chipping, and smoothing. Other recommendations include the following:

Some children begin to soften the clay in their hands while others use the nature loose parts in their clay sculptures.

Maddie, age five, illustrates her character, Prickly the porcupine.

- Cutting tools
  - dental floss
  - skewers
  - paper clips
  - pastry cutter
  - dull butter knife
- Smoothing and flattening tools
  - large jars
  - wooden and acrylic rollers
  - wooden dowels
  - hands
- Joining and texturing tools
  - toothbrush
  - loose parts
  - shoe soles, cardboard, lace, burlap, packing bubbles, and textiles
- Wire tools
  - wire cutters
  - needle-nose pliers
  - masking tape (to cover the sharp end of the wire)

Tools in the sculpture makerspace provide opportunities for children to smooth, cut, carve, and create texture in the clay.

Playdough can serve as an attachment because of the joining nature of the material. However, other attachment techniques are needed when using denser clay materials. The most common attachments that we use to reinforce joints in this makerspace are

- toothpicks and
- skewers.

A toothpick was used to attach the head to the body of this child's reindeer character.

Sculpture makerspace with natural clay and glass loose parts

Spaces for Playing and Making

This was the first time these four-year-olds had ever experienced the grainy, smooth, cool, and earthy natural clay. Pelo (2007) advocates for investing in offering natural clay to children because it "communicates our deep regard for their rights as learners and for their competence as artist[s]" (58). At first the children showed a great deal of curiosity about the new tools in the makerspace. They wondered what the tools could do and began testing and tinkering with what lines, patterns, and textures could be created as they ran the tool through the clay. With each line that passed through the material, a new image appeared in the mind of the child as the material and child conversed with each other. When William ran the wavy cutter through the clay, he said it looked like shark's teeth: "I'm going to make a shark!"

William tinkers with the clay tool and imagines shark teeth.

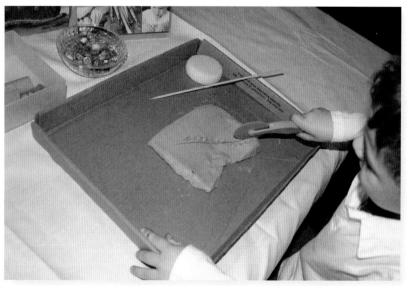

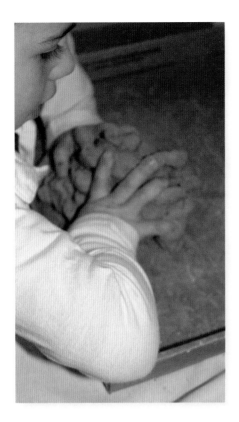

Tinkering with the clay to explore its properties and discover how it could change

With each new pinch, he imagined what the clay could become in his hands. When William stretched the clay, it evoked a memory, and he said, "Did you know that elephants have trunks?" Then, after another cut of the straight cutter tool, he said, "That looks like a bat." Then his focus shifted to inquiring about the clay itself. William used his hand muscles to pull the clay together and tinker with changing the texture and the shape. Wondering if he could change the shape again, he began pulling and tearing the clay into smaller pieces.

The children spent their first day in the new makerspace exploring the tools and the new main material. It is important not to rush or skip the beneficial stage of exploring. In the learning practices of the maker movement, these behaviors are labeled as "inquiring" and "tinkering" to learn about the properties of the materials and tools.

The next day, William went back to inquiring about the tools, but this time his focus was on the skewers. "What can we do with these?" he asked himself and continued to experiment by making holes and lines to see what would happen. This exploration into clay and tools continued over the next few days. Jill Fox and Robert Schirrmacher (2015) describe the process thus: "As scientists, they put clay to a series of tests by rolling, pinching, tearing, pulling, and poking it. By physically acting on clay they discover its properties" (260).

The next week the educator joined the group and quietly played and sculpted in the area to see what children would observe and notice. She began to make rolls with the clay. One of the children looked up and said, "That looks like it's going to be an octopus!" The educator took the idea and joined more tentacles to the main shape. William suggested that the creature be smiling and asked if he could add

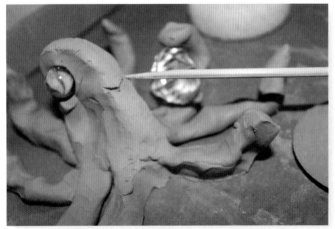

William demonstrates the learning practice of "seek and share resources" by collaborating with his educator.

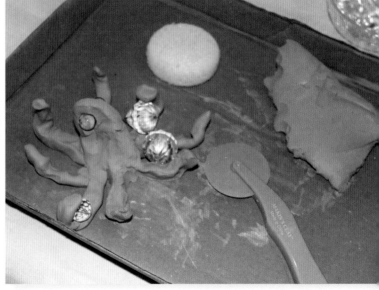

a smile to the piece. The two of them then began talking about how this could be an octopus that found a pirate's treasure. William respectfully asked to place glass "jewels" in the sculpture's arms. This was a perfect example of how a child with a strong desire to learn sought resources and knowledge from the educator about how to work with this material.

A few days later, William returned to the sculpture makerspace. He remembered the wavy cutting tool and what it made him think of when he made his first line in the natural clay. He expressed his intention, saying, "I think I'm going to make a shark today!" He repurposed the clay shapes he had made the previous day and cut a chunk of clay and made the fin. Then he used his full body to pound and smooth the pieces of clay together to form the body, attached the tail with a skewer, and then formed two side fins to complete his main shark shape. He chose marbles to represent the eyes and finally went back to the tool that inspired his making. He rolled the wavy cutter tool back and forth to give his shark teeth. William demonstrated a growing fluency with the materials and tools in making something that was meaningful to him.

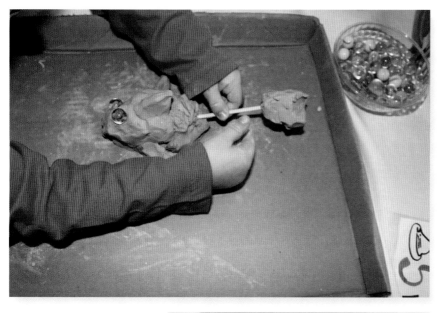

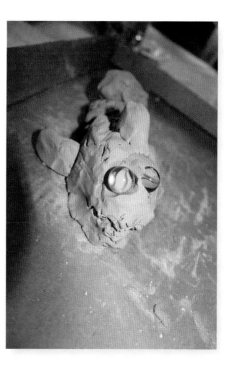

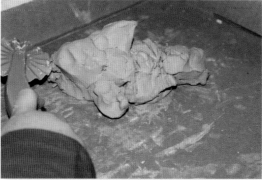

William returns to the clay to make his imagined shark character, using all the tools and attachment methods he was exposed to over time.

Documenting Learning in the Sculpture Makerspace

Learning Practices that Lead to the Development of a Maker Mindset	Indicators of Learning through Enactment of the Practices
Inquire	• William wondered what the tools could do and explored how he could change the clay by making lines and patterns with the tool. • William asked questions about how to use the skewers.
Tinker	• William pinched, pulled, and tore pieces of clay with his hands to change the texture and the shape.
Seek and Share Resources	• William collaborated to make the octopus sculpture and shared ideas with others.
Hack and Repurpose	• William repurposed his sculpture from the previous day to form the fin and body of the shark he had imagined making.
Express Intent	• After connecting the wavy line he made with the cutter to what he knew about shark's teeth, William stated that he was going to make a shark.
Develop Fluency	• William practiced with the skewers and added details of a smile to the collaborative sculpture. • William continued to work with clay over time and began to smooth and attach pieces together as he made his shark.
Simplify to Complexify	• William used glass jewels to represent a story of a pirate's treasure. • William combined pieces of clay and marbles to represent his shark idea.

More Sculpture Makerspaces to Inspire Your Making

Developing fluency in the different sculpting materials and tools takes time. Therefore, children need time and varying exposure throughout the year to fully explore the properties of each material and gain the confidence and ability they need to act on an idea they want to sculpt in the makerspace. Here are more sculpture makerspaces to inspire you as you imagine places where children can play and make with a variety of materials. These examples follow the continuum above as the children study the properties of specific materials over the course of the year.

Playdough makerspace with nature
loose parts

Found materials makerspace with
paper loose parts

Paper sculpture technique posters displayed at The Muse Knoxville children's museum

Foil makerspace with textile loose parts

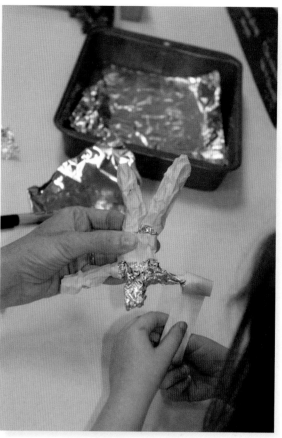

Emerson, age five, covers her delicate foil sculpture with tape to mold the features and then uses the loose parts to design clothing to match her imagined idea.

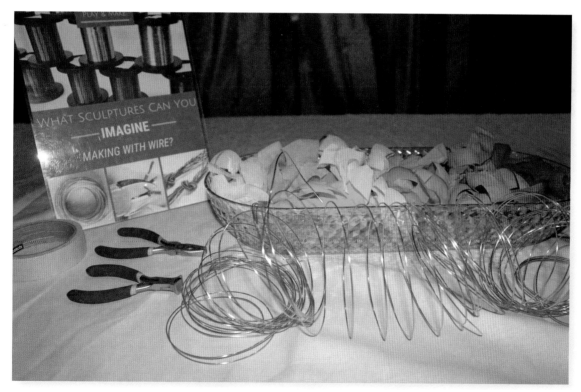

Wire makerspace with paper loose parts

Children play and make in the Squishy Circuits makerspace with plastic LED loose parts. A magical snowman that needs his light to stay frozen, a pet tiger with glowing purple eyes, and a huge black spider are imagined, shaped, and illuminated with the conductive dough.

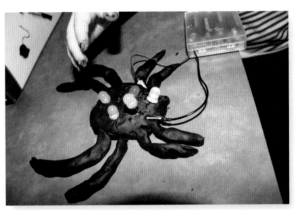

Making a Mark by reusing plastic loose parts and creating something beautiful to show responsible decision-making with materials and to be good stewards of our planet

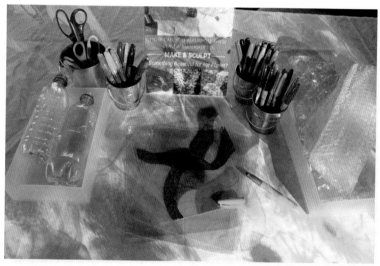

I can roll balls of clay.

I can squeeze the clay.

I can roll snakes with clay.

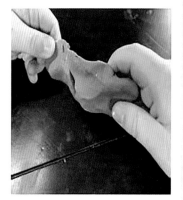

I can pull to shape the clay.

Clay techniques anchor chart to build with the children and place in the makerspace as support

Play and Make

Document the learning practices children exhibit while making by highlighting behaviors observed, using the Learning Practices Documentation form (see appendix B). Take notes on what children say and do. When children are using the material for the first time, are they tinkering with the clay? Watch for children arranging the clay to form different shapes and discover how they might fit together. As makers gain experience, watch for children hacking and repurposing the clay, tools, and/or loose parts, using them in new ways to represent ideas.

Share

Find a child who tried the new techniques and ask them to share successes or difficulties in a maker talk with the group to develop the maker mindset of sharing and collaborating. Have the child bring their sculpture and the tool they used and ask them to explain the tool's use to the class. Have the child demonstrate what the tool can do with a piece of clay. The rest of the children can think and then share how this helped them grow as sculptors and what they can now do in this makerspace.

In the sculpture makerspace, we use children's books to introduce the many types of sculptures as well as explore what clay can become when we shape and mold the materials. Books that we have used in our sculpture makerspaces include the following:

When Clay Sings by Byrd Baylor
Clay by Mary Firestone
The Little Clay Pot by Cheryl Kincaid
Claymates by Dev Petty
The Magic of Clay by Adalucía Quan
Look! Look! Look! at Sculpture by Nancy Elizabeth Wallace

Next Steps in Transforming Spaces

The continuum of materials is especially helpful in developing sculpture makerspaces because children need more modeling and practice to gain fluency in the main materials and tools. Given time and space to fully explore and learn in this makerspace, children will make great progress in developing a maker mindset.

After you have set up your first sculpture makerspace, observed children in it, and collected evidence of the learning practices of the maker movement in action, pause to reflect on and analyze how they are growing as makers. For example, if you observe children encountering difficulties and persisting by modifying their design, they are hacking and repurposing and, in turn, enacting a growth mindset. Take a moment to have a maker talk with your colleagues and reflect on how your children are growing as makers. Then collaborate on the next transformation of your sculpting makerspaces.

- What learning practices have you observed children displaying while playing and making in the sculpture makerspace? How are these behaviors connected to the maker mindset?
- Ask your children, "What have you learned about becoming a maker? What new skills do you have as a sculptor?" Reflect on how this is connected to the maker mindset.
- What is your plan for transforming your playdough area or STEAM sculpting activities with children?

PLAY & MAKE

WHAT CAN YOU IMAGINE

MAKING

WITH THESE PERFORMANCE

MATERIALS?

An invitation for children to imagine, play, and make with performance materials

CHAPTER 6

Performance Makerspaces

Dreaming characters for us to be,
Tinkering with scarves, ideas set free.
Designing costumes, settings for me,
I play and perform for all to see.

Stories to Inspire Making

The sun shone brightly as the children took their learning out into a beautiful day. The materials sparkled in the light, calling out to the children. Eager hands reached for the main attraction, a collection of sheer and shimmering scarves that almost glittered in the sun, like a "rainbow."

The ribbons ranged in color and texture from ribbed fluorescent yellow to beaded metallic gold trim to rustic twine. There was kelly-green lace, embroidery thread of every color under the sun, and fabrics galore. The denim, cotton, and silk fabrics,

Inspiration in an array of colors for costume design with textile loose parts

An outdoor performance makerspace for costume design

both solid and patterned, had their own unique textures. Thick pipe cleaners that looked like they were made of feathers and natural twine served as attachments. The sign invited the children to imagine a character they could make with the materials. Gleeful, the children touched the fabrics, held them to the light, played with them, and experimented with different ways to use them.

The materials appealed to a wide range of interests, as they were open-ended and invited children to conjure up costume ideas for themselves as well as their puppets. Ajani, five years old, wanted to be Batman, but he didn't want a black cape. His favorite color was green, so he decided to be a green Batman. He chose green lace for his headband and attached it with green pipe cleaners. He selected a green scarf as his cape and secured it with twine. He decorated his cape with green pipe cleaners. He even chose green scissors!

Ajani chooses to be a green Batman character.

Harper, six years old, wanted to be Captain Marvel, "but a girl who likes pink and purple." She chose a pink scarf and tied her pipe cleaners in a knot in the front of her cape. She twisted pipe cleaners with metallic ribbon to make her crown.

Even though she was finished with her costume, she wasn't finished being inspired by the materials. Materials create meeting places, gather children around them, and become part of our early childhood experiences, histories, and lives (Kind 2014). Harper wanted to play with them a bit more and get to know them

Harper makes a puppet character and participates in a collaborative puppet show.

Harper chooses to be a pink and purple Captain Marvel.

better. She decided she wanted to make a "sidekick," so she tinkered some more, selected a floral fabric, and designed a puppet character to accompany her in her adventures. Harper served as a resource for others who also decided to make puppets, which led to another idea: a puppet show!

Open-ended materials in this makerspace appealed equally to girls and boys and supported all ideas that emerged from the colors, textures, shapes, forms, and functions. Playing with the materials, tinkering with possibilities, and using each other as resources for their thinking, the children imagined themselves as superheroes and created puppets as companions to their new identities.

Costume design with textile loose parts

Why Is Performance the Next Makerspace to Introduce to Children?

We define the performance makerspace as a place for the *enactment* of stories, ideas, and projects. This includes dramatic play, costume design, character development, set design, action, and props. Opportunities to create entire productions invite testing, iterating, and tinkering with materials to create what was imagined.

Representation of everyday events with action, dialogue, character development, and context moves sculpture and the other makerspaces to the realm of performance. "Children's play worlds are storied worlds with texts filled with vibrant dialogue, characters, and storylines. During play, children make their own imaginary versions of real-life or fantasy worlds but on their own terms" (Wohlwend 2013, vii). We've observed children zooming around a classroom with their airplane structures or wearing their dress-up outfits in the construction makerspace to direct traffic in the imaginary city they've constructed. Although performances can take place in any makerspace, we provide explicit inspiration, focus lessons, materials, tools, and attachments to support interdisciplinary performance and its accompanying actions, characters, and contexts in the performance makerspace. Although performances can be solo, the performance makerspace is a socially constructed space that celebrates collaborative actions and ideas that are developed by small groups of interested children. "Even inanimate objects—tools, technologies, materials, and environments—may participate in the development of creative ideas" (Clapp 2017, 41).

Remaking Housekeeping and Dramatic Play Areas into a Performance Makerspace

Housekeeping areas can be found in both formal and informal learning spaces. These areas traditionally have some sort of kitchen equipment, a table with chairs, and some costumes (doctor, firefighter). Props and costumes alike have prescribed uses and cannot easily represent different ideas and thinking. Further, the items offered in these areas are not representative of real tools and materials (plastic stethoscopes, utensils, and food). Commercial puppets sometimes found in this area tend to represent specific characters and cannot be easily changed or reinvented as different characters by the children.

Research shows that children are capable of transforming ordinary objects and situations into "imaginary situations in which objects can be reimagined and remade" (Rainville and Gordh 2016, 76). Use the following chart to engage that potential. We recommend starting with character development (costumes, puppets), but a collaborative project (clubhouse, mural) builds community and can also be a good starting point.

Designing Your First Performance Makerspace

Inspiration and Support	• Children's book(s) displaying strong characters or detailed illustrations of settings/places; read and set out a copy for inspiration (*Dress Like a Girl* by Patricia Toht is a fun book to inspire possibilities for costumes and characters.) • Makerspace sign to encourage making ("What can you imagine making with performance materials?") • Focus lesson on character design (puppets) or collaborative setting (clubhouse or mural)
Main Materials	• Paper is always a good place to start. Cardboard can make a clubhouse or be used for a character, costume piece, or mural. • Fabric pieces and scarves can serve many purposes (dress-up, stage curtains).
Loose Parts	• Small, open-ended loose parts that you already have can be used to embellish and add details to characters, settings, and costumes (buttons, shells, sequins).
Tools and Attachments	• Scissors, small hands, glue. Gluing loose parts to cardboard pieces (ripped or cut) provides opportunities for discussing and thinking about details.

Before and after of the transformation from housekeeping area to emerging performance makerspace

Once your children start to play and make in the performance makerspace, use the continuum below to determine next steps with materials, dialogue, and digital apps.

Maker's Continuum of Playing and Making for Performance

Arts and Crafts

High Tech

Children are introduced to first-person narrative, designing characters, costumes, and sets for their play (puppets, dress-up, kitchen, bakery, restaurant, house, park).

As they engage in dialogue and add action to their play, they develop and design characters using third-person dialogue.

Common main materials for characters, sets, and costumes can include the following:

- cardboard
- craft sticks
- twigs
- scarves, fabric pieces
- authentic tools (silverware, oven mitts, cereal boxes)

Children design more elaborate costumes, sets, props, and characters using their imaginations and new tools (nails, hammers, low-temperature glue guns) to build more complex structures and characters as they play and make.

They use more open-ended materials and decrease the use of closed-ended materials (commercial puppets, plastic kitchen utensils).

Children engage with more high-tech apps for action (stop motion studio), setting (green screen by DoInk), and opportunities for coding the movement of character (Ozobots) and the development of digital characters (Toca Mini, ChatterPix Kids).

Kitchen equipment and dress-up costumes (doctor, fireman) are removed and children create their own characters, sets, costumes, and contexts (bakery, pizza restaurant, park).

Adaptation for the Youngest Makers

Our youngest children may initially need concrete representations for their play. We recommend using the actual objects (silverware, hats) rather than a toy version when possible. Slowly scaffold toward open-ended materials that require abstract thinking and representation.

Adaptations for Makers with Special Rights

As you move away from concrete representations for characters and settings, students with special rights may still benefit from seeing pictures of characters (firefighters, doctors) or settings (beach, restaurant) to provide the scaffolding they initially need to represent by replication.

STREAM Learning in the Performance Makerspace

Makers in the performance area have ample opportunities for STREAM learning. The chart below highlights opportunities for interdisciplinary learning and provides question stems for deep thinking across the curriculum.

Prompts to Ensure STREAM Learning Connections

Science	Makers will do the following: • Use their senses to figure out push/pull for movement and action of props ("How are you going to move/add action to your character?")
Technology	• Figure out how to use new tools and applications ("How will you use these tools/apps as you play and make characters/settings/costumes with these materials?")
Reading/Literacy	• Communicate with others ("How will you use dialogue/scripts/puppet shows to communicate with others?")
Engineering	• Develop alternative solutions ("How can you make it work with these materials?" or "How can you connect the pieces to make them go together for your play/setting/character?")
Arts	• Communicate meaning in many ways ("How did you make your costume/character/setting?" "What materials did you use to make your costume/character/setting?")
Mathematics	• Measure, recognize shapes, and count as they create costumes, sets, and characters ("How did you decide on the size/shape/details of your costume/setting/character?")

Imagine Making a Performance Makerspace

The purpose of the performance makerspace is to introduce new materials to further develop performance identities as children make robust characters, play a variety of roles, create sets, and figure out action for their stories, ideas, and characters. For this makerspace the children were making characters and focusing on adding details (physical attributes, embellishment, colors, personalities) to their characters. Our goal was to encourage elaboration as the children added loose parts to enhance their characters' looks, personalities, and actions. We also encouraged increased vocabulary (*metal*, *glisten*) and oral language as the children joined their characters in performances, conversations, stories, and play.

Performance makerspace with metal loose parts to imagine and make characters.
1. Inspiration and support (book and sign)
2. Main material (foil)
3. Loose parts (metal: pipe cleaners, nuts and bolts, mirrors) 4. Tools and attachments (glue, scissors, paper clips, clothespins)

INSPIRATION AND SUPPORT

Children entering the makerspace found inspiring and intriguing materials, including metallic pipe cleaners, small mirrors, and foil. A sign invited them to explore the metal loose parts, asking, "What character can you imagine designing with metal materials?" The book *Dress Like a Girl* showed lots of characters with different outfits, attributes, and actions to inspire the children in the design of their characters.

MAIN MATERIAL

We introduced foil as the main material in this makerspace. The children had never played with it before, and they had fun sculpting characters with it. Vivian Paley writes that "young children need to act out their thoughts to further their understanding of the world around them" (quoted in Masterson and Bohart 2019, 50). Whether used in dramatic play, set design, or prop design, main materials should be chosen to represent the thinking and forward intentions and goals of the children. Combine main materials from the previous makerspaces to expand the possibilities:

- papers and art mediums from the arts makerspace for drawing and painting scenes
- cardboard, tubes, and blocks from the construction makerspace for building sets
- playdough, clay, and wire sculptures to serve as props in dramatic play and set design
- any other open-ended main materials that might serve the purposes and imaginations of the children

Lori designed a dog character, using foil for its body.

The making of the clubhouse was a collaborative effort in which all played and made.

Every child contributed to the overall design of the clubhouse. Stephanie had decorated a round piece of card stock and wanted to hang it on the clubhouse, but she encountered a problem. The tape was in use, and she had to find another way. She located a screw. First she had to push it through her card stock circle. Even though it was difficult for her to do, she did not give up.

Stephanie selected a screw as an attachment. She first pushed it through her cardboard circle.

Next she had to find a location on the clubhouse where she could use a long screw without having it come out on the other side. She located a thick wall and pushed the screw through the cardboard, careful not to poke herself or others with it.

Stephanie persevered and pushed the screw into the clubhouse to attach the cardboard circle.

She was so proud of herself when she finished, saying, "I did it! Hooray for me!" The clubhouse looked even better with her circle attached to the front of it, with the head of the screw attesting to her efforts to learn to use a new attachment.

The children made a clubhouse out of cardboard with metal loose parts.

Documenting Learning in the Performance Makerspace

Learning Practices That Lead to the Development of a Maker Mindset	Indicators of Learning through Enactment of the Practices
Inquire	• The children asked, "What could we make?" • Stephanie walked around and asked her classmates, "What are you going to make?"
Tinker	• The children tinkered and played with how they wanted to contribute, trying out different materials and tools. • Stephanie dumped out all the metal loose parts and explored possibilities for their uses.
Seek and Share Resources	• The children used each other as resources, asking questions and getting advice for embellishing the clubhouse. • Once Stephanie figured out how to attach her plate to the clubhouse, she shared her newfound knowledge with her classmates.
Hack and Repurpose	• As a group, they decided to hack and repurpose the collaborative design and created a peephole with a metal washer. • The tape was in use, and Stephanie had to find another way to attach her circle to the clubhouse. She used a screw in an innovative way.
Express Intent	• The class decided together to make a clubhouse, and that is exactly what they did! • Stephanie exclaimed, "I need to put this on that."
Develop Fluency	• As a group, the children developed fluency with the use of the oil pastels to add color and details to the clubhouse, using them to outline, color, and write. • As Stephanie worked with the screw, trying to figure out how to push it through the cardboard, she manipulated it more easily with each attempt.
Simplify to Complexify	• This clubhouse was a simple construction but was inclusive and celebrated the talents and skills that each child brought to the project.

More Performance Arts Makerspaces to Inspire Your Making

Performance makerspaces are, quite literally, limited only by your children's imaginations. You can remix and repurpose materials from other makerspaces or inspire with new open-ended materials, from simple fabric pieces and blocks to high-tech tools. The following examples are just a few of the endless possibilities!

Exploration of costume design with cardboard and wood loose parts

Exploration of character development with wood and textile loose parts

Exploration of set design with butcher paper and paper loose parts

Exploration of character design with paper and craft materials

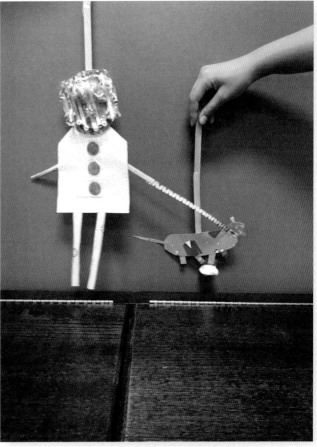

Exploration of character action with stop-motion app

Exploration of prop design with shadow show
and wood materials

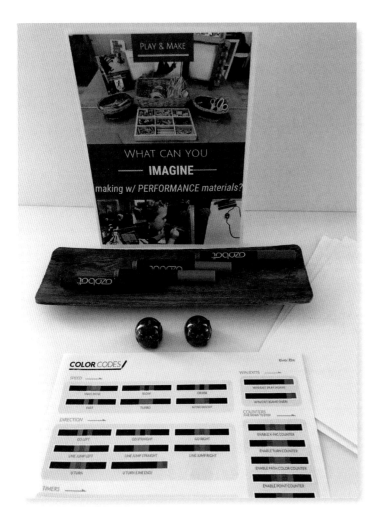

Exploration of character action with
Ozobots at Soar in 4 family events

Making a Mark during dramatic play, children demonstrate relationships with peers by working together to act out a play they imagined and made

Sharing Our Thinking

Objective: Children will imagine new ways to play with cardboard by making a special costume.

MATERIALS

- book to show ideas for costume design (We used *Dream You'll Be* by Joseph T. Garcia)
- masking tape
- paints (We used OOLY Chunkies Paint Sticks)
- cardboard pieces (cut into different sizes and shapes) and boxes
- camera for documentation

Focus and Explore

Connect: *"I have been watching you play in the dress-up area, and you seem to have a lot of fun. I noticed that sometimes you pretend you are a veterinarian or a doctor or a firefighter. That gave me an idea! I thought it might be fun to make some of the* *other people that you pretend about, like nurses or princesses or superheroes. So today we will imagine new ways to play with cardboard by making a special costume."*

Teach: *"When I was reading this book,* Dream You'll Be, *I noticed how many characters I can become. I noticed an astronaut, a rock star, and even a scientist."* Show the pages of the book and have children label ideas they could make. *"I was wondering how I can use these paper materials to help me make a costume."* Have some small pieces of cardboard cut into various sizes and shapes ready. *"Watch me as I imagine how to play differently with these materials to make a costume I want to play in."* Model placing the cardboard pieces in different arrangements to show open exploration through play. Put a piece across your face like a mask and say, *"Oh, I could make a mask!"* Pick up another piece of cardboard and look at it in wonder. Place it on your arm, like a sleeve, talking out loud to help children imagine possibilities. *"I think this piece of cardboard on my arm looks like a sleeve. Or a bracelet! I might use the loose parts to decorate it, and it can be a princess bracelet. Or it can be armor to protect me. Let me see what else I can play and make."* Continue picking up pieces of cardboard and pretending to use them for other parts of a costume (shield, wings, halo). Share your thinking out loud as you imagine the possibilities of what you could make. Hold up a piece of cardboard and say, *"This reminds me of the shape of a wing. I could make a pair of wings and be a bird. Or I could be a bumblebee. Or a fairy in the garden."*

Active Involvement: Show the children the two to three new materials you are placing in their performance makerspace along with the cardboard. Pass them around so each child can hold the objects, or put them on the overhead projector so they can examine the details as a whole group. *"Now look closely. What costume can you imagine making with these materials?"* Share or chart their ideas to help launch their making for the day.

Imagine
Ask the children to pause and think about what materials they want to explore today. Ask, *"What do you imagine making with these performance materials?"* Record their intentions for making and the makerspace they choose for the day on the Class at a Glance form (see appendix C).

Play and Make
Document the learning practices children exhibit while making by taking pictures and dictation, using the Learning Practices Documentation form (see appendix B). Take notes on what the children say and do. If you see them looking through the cardboard and playing around with it, they are inquiring and wondering about what to make. If they study the cardboard and try out different things, they are

tinkering. If you notice the children folding, cutting, or using the cardboard in unusual ways, they are hacking and repurposing.

Share

Find a child who used a new material and ask them to share with the group in a maker talk to inspire future makers in the performance makerspace. Ask the children what they plan to do next in their making. This is a good practice to get children in the habit of expressing intentions and developing goals.

SUGGESTED BOOKS TO INSPIRE MAKERS WITH PERFORMANCE

In the performance makerspace, we use a lot of children's books that show structures for set designs and detailed characters for character development. This list of recommended titles includes notes on books that are useful for specific elements of performance:

A Season to Bee: A Stylish Book of Color by Carlos Aponte
The Curious Garden by Peter Brown (setting; set design)
Recipe for a Story by Ella Burfoot
Do Princesses Wear Hiking Boots? by Carmela LaVigna Coyle
Ladybug Girl and the Dress-Up Dilemma by Jacky Davis
The Paper Dolls by Julia Donaldson
Dream You'll Be by Joseph T. Garcia
Fraidyzoo by Thyra Heder
A Great Cake by Tina Matthews (using cooking props in an open-ended way)
Use Your Imagination by Nicola O'Byrne
Dress Like a Girl by Patricia Toht
With My Hands: Poems about Making Things by Amy VanDerwater
   (shadow show)

Next Steps in Transforming Spaces

In this intentional performance makerspace, your children will imagine, play, make, and share characters, sets, costumes, and more. As you transform your performance makerspace, introducing more complex main materials and loose parts to scaffold and inspire, make sure your performance makerspace maintains the components of a developing maker mindset. Consider innovation across content areas: this makerspace offers everything from drawing ideas on paper to building costumes to using them in performances—from idea to action—or from being characters (in dramatic play) to designing, scripting, and directing ideas in animated productions. As your children play and make, document their enactment of the learning practices to analyze their development of their maker mindsets.

For example, if you observe children going from space to space, collecting materials for their productions and costumes, they are seeking and sharing resources and hacking and repurposing materials from other makerspaces. As they cross domains, they are becoming STREAM innovators, one of the characteristics of a maker mindset.

Pause and reflect with your colleagues on the habits of mind your children are developing as they develop maker mindsets through playing and making in the performance makerspace.

- Where will you begin the transformation of your performance makerspace? (character development, set design, costume design, prop development)
- How can you make your performance makerspace a space for collaborative thinking and playing? What are some ideas for performances?
- What learning practices have you observed children displaying while playing and making in the performance makerspace? Which aspects of these behaviors are connected to building a maker mindset?
- Ask your children, "What have you learned about becoming a maker?" "What new skills do you have as a performer?" Reflect on how their answers are connected to the maker mindset.

WHAT SMALL WORLDS CAN YOU

— IMAGINE —

MAKING WITH THESE MATERIALS?

An invitation for children to imagine, play, and make in a small world makerspace

CHAPTER 7

Small World Makerspaces

SMALL WORLD

Crafting worlds, mixing sand, mud, or slime,
I form landscapes from all different times.
Messes are made, ideas swirl about.
Residents invented, live here throughout.
A universe full of possibilities
now planted, rooted, a world for me.

Stories to Inspire Making

The children, ages two to four, wondered at the shades of lime green, milky white, and vivid aqua glowing from the clear containers filled with a new and watery globe-shaped material. Images of green landscapes, cold winter days, and the depths of the deep blue sea surfaced in discussions of the small world makerspace. As the children began exploring the water beads, they were drawn to the glow of the colors, accentuated by a light table. The children drew on their memories to imagine habitats, and they explored the materials by dumping all the colored water beads together. Exploring new materials is an important part of the making process in which children discover the properties of objects and learn what they can do (Topal and Gandini 1999). As the water beads spilled onto the floor, the children squished the beads with their hands and bare feet, feeling the water seep out and

An invitation for children to create a small world from their
imaginations by using a new material of water beads

Children explore the properties of the water beads, interacting with the material to imagine new possibilities to make.

smashing some into tiny parts. They were struck by how small they could make the pieces and how the edges shined in the light. "Wow, this looks like tiny gems!" one child said as he poked at the crushed, backlit water beads. They were making a bit of a mess, but a universe of ideas and possibilities swirled in their heads.

The children then approached the wooden loose parts, curious about if and how they would float on top of the "sea" of water beads. A pile of craft sticks, clothespins,

While inquiring about the materials, the child discovered that the beads were strong enough to hold the wood materials on the surface. He imagined the material as water.

and sticks began to form, and then a child said, "It looks like they're floating on water!" He then began flipping through a book with habitat scenes and found a river image with the same sea-green shade of water that he wanted to ponder. Exploring materials unleashes a child's imagination and invites children to tell stories (Topal and Gandini 1999).

The river image became a teaching and inspirational material in this small world makerspace as the child repurposed the sticks to form a home for living creatures. With each interaction with the child, the materials are in a process of transformation, about to become something different (Taguchi 2011). The rough-textured sticks transformed into a burrow. The clothespins attached at varying angles transformed into river otters. Together the making of the child and properties of the materials created a watery landscape with wood-eating residents where the child could play and perform the everyday events of the small world he had invented.

Materials transform into a river dwelling for a family of river otters.

Why Is Small World the Next Makerspace to Introduce to Children?

When children have acted out their thoughts in set design, costume creation, and character development in performance makerspaces, they begin to visualize how all those pieces come together to create a beautiful world or story. Creating innovative worlds is one of the goals of our small world makerspace. Watch the director's commentary notes at the end of a movie and you will hear how many fine details, from the texture of the clothing to the design of a set, came together to tell a story. Each element added to the director's world had a purpose: to relate an experience to an audience. When children play with sensory materials, they experience a variety of perspectives and take on the role of the director creating the world, as well as the actors, as they make and put their stories into words (Smith 2012). All five senses can be engaged in making an imagined scene or small world. Playing with textures, design, form, and possibilities in pretend and real-world experiences builds along a continuum, becoming more complex throughout the year.

Remaking a Sensory Area into a Small World Makerspace

When we first analyzed the sensory centers in preschool classrooms and sensory science-related activities throughout the elementary grades (making slime, Oobleck), we found that the areas offered only one main material and the same tools during the experiment or over time. The focus was on exploring the properties of the material, but children had little opportunity to unleash their imaginations and make beyond the predetermined uses of the sensory materials or the experiment directions. For example, sand tables usually contained the same funnel, sifting, and shaping toys for as long as the sand table was a center. At times, plastic figurines were added to the space to increase play. However, figurines and sand molds expressed only the character they were intended to be: a dolphin would remain a dolphin and a starfish a starfish throughout play.

Adaptations for Makers with Special Rights

Including concrete objects in play is an important strategy for supporting very young children and children with communication difficulties. You may want to begin with a variety of plastic figurines or clip art pictures so children have an opportunity to choose characters before working up to making them with loose parts. This also provides a nice scaffold to understanding what children are making in their small worlds.

After playing and exploring the properties of the playdough, an eighteen-month-old child selected a lion figurine. He began acting out trying to pull his lion out of the "mud," saying, "Uhhh, stuck."

In learning centers and homes encouraging small world play, the story to be re-enacted was established by adults or set by the choice of figurines placed in the area. There is nothing wrong with establishing small world play in this fashion because any form of play benefits children in their growth and learning. We encourage playing and making the first small worlds together to help children imagine possibilities during focus lessons. However, when children are familiar with small worlds, you can transform your small world play areas into makerspaces. Provide more open-ended materials and prompts for children to use as they imagine and make small worlds and their inhabitants. This gives most of the thinking and making back to the child, who can then tinker with ideas and hack and repurpose materials to make the scene *they* imagine. In doing so, children draw on their learning across all subject areas to foster quality interdisciplinary thinking and STREAM innovation. Further, "kinesthetic learners who are given the opportunity to build in order to think, and language-disabled students who can show visually their thinking in order to communicate, begin to regard themselves as contributing members of the classroom community, as having something to say, as possessing ideas and imagination" (Smith 2012, 49).

We therefore define small world play as making a life scene as an invitation for children to play with sensory materials. Small worlds grow from many themes, shapes, materials, and displays: if you or your children can imagine it, it is possible to make! The goal is for children to act out ideas from their imagination or real life, share facts about a topic they know well, or retell their favorite stories. By making three-dimensional small worlds, "experience, event, memory, and emotion can be shown, sorted out, and communicated" (Smith 2012, 20). Let's start with a small world makerspace using a common main material, such as sand, that will help you begin transforming your sensory learning spaces.

Designing Your First Small World Makerspace

Inspiration and Support	• Children's book(s) showing images of different habitats; read and set out copies for inspiration. A great introduction to habitats can be found in the book *Welcome Home, Bear*, or use a book or pictures of landscapes that you may already have. • Makerspace sign to encourage making ("What places can you imagine making with these sensory materials?") • Focus lesson inquiring about what kinds of habitats there are to make. Highlight examples from the book and chart with describing words (green grass, cold snow).
Main Materials	• Any sensory material you have available. Sand, rice, and beans are good starting points. Children will imagine it as the ground of a habitat they are exploring.
Loose Parts	• Nature objects, as you will be highlighting outdoor habitats. Moss, raffia, sticks, and rocks are good initial offerings.
Tools and Attachments	• Scoops for children to use in exploring and moving the material to make the ground of their imagined landscapes.

After setting up your first small world makerspace, revisit the continuum of materials below to refresh it throughout the year. Use it as a support as you transition into new ways of playing and making, from the arts-and-crafts entry point described above to creating digital inhabitants with robotics or landscapes with technology, such as augmented reality.

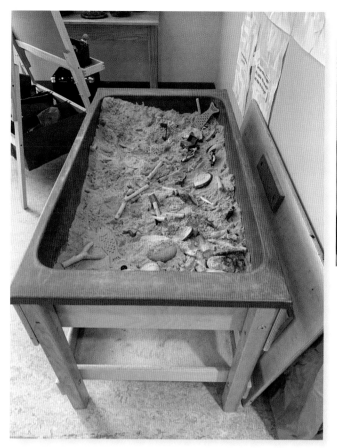

Before and after of the first transformation from sensory area to emerging small world makerspace

Maker's Continuum of Playing and Making Small Worlds

Arts and Crafts

←——————————————————————————————————→

High Tech

Children select a figurine and make the small world they imagine by choosing a main material (sand, paper, felt, light) on which to design the habitat, home, or landscape they imagine.	Children use loose parts and take apart machines to repurpose parts to build characters and/or small worlds, then they choose a main material to design the habitat, home, or landscape they imagine.	Children engineer biomechanical animals, code robots, or program 3-D printers to make inhabitants to interact with the small world they created with loose parts or in a digital world.

STREAM Learning in the Small World Makerspace

Playing in a small world makerspace promotes strong STREAM connections to learning. Children draw on their science knowledge of habitats, animals, and what living things need to survive to make the details of their small worlds. But that is just the beginning of the STREAM connections children can make as they invent their own small worlds. Use the prompts below in the small world makerspace to ensure connections across disciplines and standards across the content area studies.

Prompts to Ensure STREAM Learning Connections

Science	Makers will do the following: • Use their five senses to explore the form and function of the sensory material ("Explain how this material looks/sounds/feels/smells. How can you use the material to make a habitat/landscape/place?")
Technology	• Use measuring tools to quantify how much they need of a material to represent the landscape they are making ("What is the best tool to use to measure how much you need of this material?")
Reading/Literacy	• Develop their language abilities when narrating their play and use vocabulary inspired by the objects they touch ("What words can you use to describe the parts of the place you are making?")
Engineering	• Design models to represent real or imaginary places ("What materials do you need to make your place? Why would that make the best ground for the people or animals that live there?")
Arts	• Use their sense of touch to evaluate what kind of texture they want to add to their small world ("Describe how you want your small world to look and feel [bumpy, rough, smooth]. Which materials do you need to make what you imagine?")
Mathematics	• Measure the amount of main material you will need to cover the ground of your container. ("How much will you need to make the ground of your small world?")

Imagine Making a Small World Makerspace

The purpose of this small world makerspace was to develop makers' identities through opportunities to become inventors of their own worlds. They would also grow as artists as they examined the art element texture to select materials that would describe what the landscape looked like in their imagination. Children verbally shared what place they had imagined and made, which increased their storytelling abilities.

Small world makerspace with natural loose parts: 1. Inspiration and support (books and sign) 2. Main material (playdough) 3. Loose parts (natural stones, moss, flowers) 4. Tools and attachments (dough stampers)

In planning this makerspace, we first reflected on the interests of the children in this learning environment. They live near the Great Smoky Mountains National Park, and many of them had visited the area. They had recently discovered a book in the classroom on different parks and began asking questions and studying different images. The makerspace thus invited them to design their own park or setting from their imagination, inspired by photographs and images of the wildlife that might live in these varying worlds. Since this was the first time children would be creating a small world, we reminded them of their ability to persist in their ideas. We included a favorite storytime book about forest creatures and encouraged them to tinker with the materials until they made what they had imagined—displaying a growth mindset. If you plan to invite children to tell stories or write about events from real life or topics they know a lot about, include photographs, informational texts, or posters in the space. Whatever your intent, this first decision of planning your purpose for making should drive the selection of the rest of your materials in the small world makerspace.

Inspiring worlds from a character tinkering and making, along with scenes from national parks, which the children have been investigating

MAIN MATERIAL

In most small world spaces, the landscape drives your selection of the main material. Ask yourself, "What will the landscape look like based on our curricular goals or the children's interest?" For example, this makerspace offered playdough in selected shades of green and brown to echo the colors of the national park images provided. We added pine and spruce essential oils to the dough so children could imagine the forest elements coming to life.

If you are investigating the Arctic, white shredded paper, cloud dough, or even ice could be your main material. If children are interested in the sea or pond life, water beads, colored water, or sand could be the foundation of their small worlds.

Here are a few more landscape ideas to help you imagine possibilities for your main material:

- house
- space, lunar surface
- construction site
- forest, woodland, jungle
- park, backyard
- under the sea
- beach, lake, pond
- farm
- castle
- train station, airport

Another option is to select a main material and observe as the creativity of the children emerges. Children always come up with unexpected new ideas, and a material can bring out an experience or idea they want to share. A main material landscape of black beans could conjure images of space or a recent experience gardening in the dark dirt. When children explore and mess around with a material in their hands, they imagine a universe of possibilities. Here are some suggestions for main materials for your small world makerspaces:

- playdough in various colors (add essential oils or dried flowers to increase sensory experience)
- cloud dough
- dyed rice
- dried beans (black, split peas, kidney, lentils)
- corn
- kinetic sand or play sand
- water beads
- water or ice
- chalkboard

- light table
- fabric, felt, or wool
- dirt or grass
- seeds or birdseed
- small pebbles
- Oobleck
- shredded paper

One child uses different shades of green to create the surface of his emerging landscape. He discovers the brown playdough and molds it to form a volcano.

LOOSE PARTS

Most designers of small worlds add animals or figurines to the space at this point. In most learning areas, figurines are used either for play or as manipulatives when learning about specific animal groups or topics. Ask yourself, "Who will the inhabitants be in the space?" If you are providing plastic figurines as a scaffold for children to play in a more concrete way, we suggest displaying them in "idea jars." These jars contain a variety of animals, people, and vehicles. If a child does not find a figurine that matches their imagination, encourage them to make with the loose parts provided.

The following list of inhabitants is a starting point for the loose parts you might pull for your small world makerspace. However, children have amazing, creative minds and will imagine just about anything with loose parts from different categories (glass, nature, paper, textiles) that you share over time. Toward the end of the maker's continuum of materials above, children begin to program 3-D printers to make the animals they imagine or even construct biomechanical animals to include and interact with the small world they have created.

- human figures (children, adults, community helpers, heroes, villains)
- fantasy figures (fairies, gnomes, dragons, mermaids)
- animals (pets, farm, zoo, wild, fish, birds, reptiles, insects, mammals, prehistoric creatures)
- transportation (cars, trains, planes, boats, space, construction equipment)

If you do not already have these figurines in your learning space, or if you want children to represent their thinking in a more complex and abstract way, use loose parts! Instead of buying the plastic toys, we suggest pulling a specific category of loose parts that would match the landscape and character details of possible inhabitants. For example, the rocks and pine cones could easily transform into woodland creatures. In this makerspace we provided the following nature loose parts to match the overall feel of the outdoor small worlds the children might create:

- pine cones
- fresh flowers
- moss
- sticks
- river rocks

Nature loose parts to inspire details of the scene
and inhabitants that might live there

Adding tools increases the children's ability to inquire into the main material to discover what it is made of and what it can do. In this makerspace we offered wooden rollers and cookie presses to add texture to the playdough material. The most common tools used to explore the properties of sensory materials include

- scoops,
- tongs,
- funnels, and
- eyedroppers.

When children create landscapes or their inhabitants, they often need to secure pieces together. The most common attachments used in this space include

- playdough,
- twine, and
- clothespins.

Wood rollers and cookie stamps were provided to add texture to the small worlds.

Organization/Aesthetics

Consider what containers you can add to the makerspace for individual or collaborative making opportunities. Containers hold the main material representing a small world's foundation or ground. Consider the number of children in the makerspace to determine whether you need one large container or several smaller containers. For this makerspace a few children were invited to make on a large wood slice.

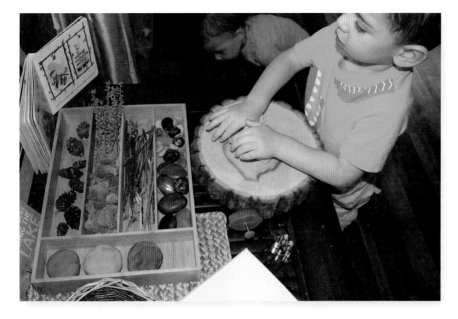

One maker spreads out his playdough on the wood slice "container" to begin tinkering with what scene he might make.

He proudly displays his completed small world of his grandma's house in the forest made of sticks.

Spaces for Playing and Making

One afternoon at The Muse Knoxville, children from ages three to nine found a new pop-up makerspace inviting them to imagine and make a landscape or home with dried beans and textile loose parts. As children trickled into the space, we shared with them pages from the book *A House in the Sky* by Steve Jenkins. The illustrations and words were powerful inspiration for the many types of homes they could make. The "How to Make a Small World" anchor chart supported the children in thinking through the process. It prompted them to think about the possibilities and then begin selecting from the two dried-bean options (split peas and black beans) and tinkering with how the main material looked in the clear plant-drip tray containers we provided. Each child could take home the small world they made.

The small world makerspace where children were prompted to think about what home they wanted to make and select the dried beans to make the ground

The children were offered two different palettes of textile loose parts so they would not feel limited in the type of home they wanted to create. Neutral tones could represent rocks, mud, or even a lunar landscape, while the cool tones inspired by another Steve Jenkins book, *Living Color*, could add details of grass, water, or sea or land creatures.

Neutral and cool color palettes of textile loose parts were provided for children to imagine a world of possibilities.

One of the first children to enter the small world makerspace was three-year-old Elijah. He was drawn to the green peas right away and made the "ground" for his home. However, he wasn't sure what he wanted to make. He scanned all the materials a few times and decided to test out how the blue glitter glue would look in his tray.

Elijah evaluates the materials displayed and selects the glitter glue to test how it looks in his small world.

At this point Elijah's mom asked him if he wanted to make a frog, since it looked like he'd just made a pond. His eyes lit up, and he said, "No, I need to make a cow." Elijah had just discovered the small world he wanted to make and expressed intention about the type of living things he envisioned in his space. He selected the cotton balls, glued them together, and then carefully placed and glued black beans to make the spots. "I need a few more spots on the cow." He beamed as he held up his completed cow and placed it in his small world. I asked him if he could share what he had made. "This is my cow. He needs water. He looks angry." I asked, "Why does he look angry?" I could tell this was sparking a story that Elijah wanted to share. Elijah smiled and said, "Because he got all muddy!" This gave him another idea, and he went back to the loose parts and selected the brown wool to repurpose as mud to enhance his small world.

Elijah expresses intention to make a cow and then repurposes the wool to enhance his small world by making "mud."

Even though all children had access to the same materials in this makerspace, they each imagined very different small worlds to make.

Anakin, age three, explores all the materials and creates a home with grass for his troll character.

Saanvi, age six, persists in her attempts to cut the ribbons and literally pushes up her sleeves to continue her hard work. In the end she creates a beautiful forest world complete with a pond and a standing tree.

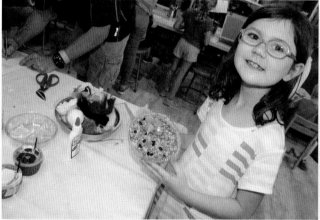

Makenzie, age seven, carefully seeks out resources to make the sea creature she imagines. She measures each piece of yarn to make similar arms for her octopus.

Learning Practices that Lead to the Development of a Maker Mindset	Indicators of Learning through Enactment of the Practices
Inquire	• Elijah was curious about the green peas and chose to play and make with that material. • All children examined the loose parts closely, deciding what to add to their small world.
Tinker	• Elijah took a risk and played with adding the blue glitter glue to his landscape, which inspired water for the cow he made. • All children played and tinkered with the materials by sprinkling the beans through their fingers and spreading them around with their hands.
Seek and Share Resources	• Elijah shared what he knew about cows by adding water details to his small world and explaining that information. • All children used the anchor chart and book, demonstrating a desire to learn how to make a small world.
Hack and Repurpose	• Elijah returned to the loose parts to look for a material that enhanced the mud detail in the story he shared. • Some children cut the loose parts to change size and shape to best represent a detail in the small world.
Express Intent	• Elijah stated that he needed to make a cow for his small world. • All children explained what they were making after spending time tinkering with the materials.
Develop Fluency	• Elijah felt confident in what he made and learned how to invent a small world with materials. • Some children discovered that they needed a sharper pair of scissors to transform the materials.
Simplify to Complexify	• Elijah combined the materials to represent the green grass and water his cow character needed to live. • All children combined different materials and loose parts to make something new and meaningful in their small worlds.

More Small World Makerspaces to Inspire Your Making

The possibilities of the small world makerspace are endless. Be sure to provide children with a variety of experiences throughout the year so they discover how different materials and tools work in different situations. You may feel overwhelmed at first, but don't worry! Start with your children's interests, curriculum topics, or a good book for inspiration. Here are a few more small world makerspaces to inspire you as you create meaningful playing and making experiences in which children can make worlds from their imaginations or represent their knowledge of life sciences.

Sand landscape with metal loose parts

When exploring the blue sand, one child said it looked like the ocean and selected an image to project that matched what he was imagining as he continued to play and make.

Kinetic sand landscape with glass loose parts

A child scoops the glass loose parts into the sand represented as water, where he imagined a pirate's treasure.

A Kodo Kids color-changing light table landscape transformed into a small world makerspace with inspiration, support, and translucent plastic loose parts at The Muse at the Mall in Knoxville, Tennessee.

A toddler tinkers with how he can make new colors with cellophane as his mom gently scaffolds his learning by asking if his blue square could be a pond, lake, or river. Children explored the plastic materials and investigated how to change the colors to imagine new landscapes.

Shredded paper landscape with metal loose parts

Brown shredded paper and inspiring images selected by the children to express the intention to make a bat cave

Water landscape with paper and recyclable loose parts

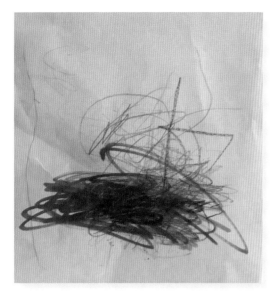

A story about a "rainbow ocean" emerges, shared through writing, as children play with the color tablets.

Engineering biomechanical animals expands children's knowledge of making inhabitants across the maker movement continuum of materials and tools. This mechanical rabbit coconstructed with a child promoted a new idea to make a small world for the rabbit to live in.

The great innovators at The Muse at the Mall in Knoxville, Tennessee, transformed dressing rooms into play spaces. We added wooden loose parts and inspiration to the Kodo Kids felt story props to design this small world makerspace.

Home by Carson Ellis

Lovely Beasts: The Surprising Truth by Kate Gardner

Above and Below by Patricia Hegarty

A House in the Sky by Steve Jenkins

Wild Ideas by Elin Kelsey

We Build Our Homes: Small Stories of Incredible Animal Architects
   by Laura Knowles

Fur, Feather, Fin—All of Us Are Kin by Diane Lang

Over and under the Pond by Kate Messner

Welcome Home, Bear: A Book of Animal Habitats by Il Sung Na

Next Steps in Transforming Spaces

By remaking your small world play or sensory areas into a small world makerspace, you allow children to be the thinkers and inventors of what the small world will look like and who will live in the homes or habitats they create. They will tinker and test out their ideas with materials, seek resources in the books and images you display for inspiration, and hack and repurpose the materials to match the small worlds from their imaginations. When you are comfortable recording evidence of the children enacting the learning practices of the maker movement, pause and reflect on how they are growing as makers of small worlds. For example, as children simplify to complexify while making a habitat with simple materials, they are applying STREAM innovation to challenges. As they imagine a home or habitat to make, they draw on their knowledge from science or social studies to create these places and develop this aspect of a maker mindset. Take a moment to have a maker talk with your colleagues and reflect on how your children are developing a maker mindset. Collaborate on the next steps in your transformation of your small world makerspaces.

- What learning practices have you observed children displaying while playing and making in the small world makerspace? How are these behaviors connected to the maker mindset?
- Ask children, "What connections have you made to other topics of study? How has that helped you become an inventor of your small world?" Reflect on how this is connected to your STREAM learning goals.
- What topics or inquiry studies can you connect to a small world makerspace? What main material(s) would you choose to support children in inventing or explaining what they know about a place?

What Can You Imagine

MAKING

WITH THESE FIBER ARTS MATERIALS?

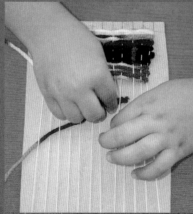

An invitation to imagine, play, and make in a fiber arts makerspace

CHAPTER 8

Fiber Arts Makerspaces

Gathering fibers to wrap, sew, or weave,
My yarn knots up, time to roll up my sleeves.
Retracing my steps and making new plans,
Up and down I go, my tools are my hands.
Beauty unfolds, I repurpose these strings.
Stitching together, this might be my thing!

Stories to Inspire Making

Children ages four to eight explored the texture of the malleable fibers and the possibilities of making in this pop-up makerspace. The balls of soft green and tan yarn displayed the muted tones of nature, and other fibers unrolled into slowly changing variations of color that the children had witnessed in *Extra Yarn* by Mac Barnett, the inspirational book for this space. In direct contrast, a pile of rigid and scaly sticks invited children to imagine ways to combine the two differing materials to make something beautiful or interesting by wrapping. Materials draw children in and can invite actions and communicate meanings (Kind 2014).

The first interaction with the materials came from a four-year-old boy who said, "I know what this is. I want to knit too." He took the sticks and began gesturing with

Introduction to fiber arts with a wrapping makerspace

One child displays his memory of knitting as another child imagines becoming a web maker.

loops of yarn to represent his memory of the character knitting in the book. He had knowledge that he could make things with this material and that items made of yarn had to be first designed by someone—a powerful first concept in children's development as creative fiber artists, weavers, and sewers. Another child selected a type of yarn and wanted to experiment. He began to wrap the yarn faster and faster around the stick and with great pride stated, "I'm a web maker! Look at the webs I can make!" Then he ran to another space in the room to share with his friends what he had made.

The child returned a few minutes later and wanted to make something else. He selected another stick from the collection and this time slowed down his motions to wrap. He was excited to watch the material build and build as he grew more familiar with the properties and functions of the yarn. He then selected another color and said, "I'm making a rainbow stick!"

Exploring the properties of yarn to make his "rainbow stick"

As more children of different genders and ages came to the makerspace, the experimenting continued. Another child slowly wrapped sticks in different shades of green and then used the pom-poms to add details of "pine cones." Another child, age eight, expressed that she wanted to make the God's-eye, or *Ojo de Dios*, that was displayed in the area for additional inspiration. She asked for more choices of yarn and selected the craft sticks that she recalled using in her previous experience. She wove over and under until, at the very end of our time, she asked for a piece of paper. We provided it, but we were curious and asked how she planned to use it in her design. Throughout her time wrapping and weaving the yarn around the sticks, her ideas had evolved into creating kites and placing her work on a canvas to proudly hang and display.

When working with fibers of any kind, there will be slow starts and knots of yarn along the way, but isn't that great? Given time to experiment with this material and guidance on learning basic techniques for a variety of fiber arts, children will run with it!

Exploring the properties of yarn to make a "rainbow stick"

This eight-year-old child explores making *Ojos de Dios* with the yarn and expresses a desire to make kites as she collects all of her pieces to place into her final piece of art.

Why Is Fiber Arts the Next Makerspace to Introduce to Children?

We define fiber arts as art made with fibers of all kinds, such as yarn, string, wool, and fabric. Fiber arts is the last category of makerspace materials and tools that we delved into, investigating ways to incorporate these materials and life skills into our formal and informal learning spaces. After children have incorporated the elements of art (color, lines, shape, texture, and design) in making with more common materials, in two and three dimensions, and then selected components to design their own three-dimensional small worlds, they are prepared to weave all of that knowledge together to make with fiber. They can design landscapes and characters while learning the more complex skills of weaving, embroidery, and sewing. Making with materials and tools in the fiber arts calls for more refined fine-motor skills, and we present a continuum of fiber arts materials throughout this chapter to help you introduce young children to the basics and complexify over time or with older children.

In visiting many middle school, high school, and adult makerspaces, we noticed a lack of fiber arts in our classrooms. In fact, the pre-K classrooms we observed offered these materials only when a specific project was being introduced by the educator and the children all made the same product. Developing fine-motor skills is an important standard in the classroom, so we also saw the use of lacing boards. While lacing is an important precursor to stitching skills, the boards featured familiar images or characters that were predetermined by the manufacturer.

The fiber arts provide many social-emotional benefits, such as helping children slow down, relax, and pay attention. Scientists have also documented that when we engage in life-sustaining activities, such as creating clothing, our bodies release dopamine and serotonin—chemicals that make us feel happy (Blum and Newman 2017). When children develop basic weaving and sewing techniques, they can not only make something useful but also represent their stories, ideas, and thinking. Therefore, we knew that this was an important makerspace to design in the play and STEAM learning areas so all children have an opportunity to investigate the fiber arts.

Remaking a Lacing Area or Fiber Projects Area into a Fiber Arts Makerspace

We observed children engaging initially with the lacing activities, but as they focused on the up-and-down motions, they did not engage their imaginations. Starting children with wrapping and then moving them on to cutting their own creatures or shapes and punching holes where they want to thread increases their ability to tinker, hack, and repurpose with fibers and was thus our first step in transforming our spaces. When introducing children to this new and diverse landscape of materials, start with something simple and open-ended to uncover their interests, abilities, and previous knowledge of working with fibers. The sample makerspace design below will inspire you to begin your first transformation and introduce children to fiber arts.

Designing Your First Fiber Arts Makerspace

Inspiration and Support	• Children's book(s) showing characters interacting with fibers; read and set out copies for inspiration. Barnett's *Extra Yarn* shows how the texture and color of yarn can make ordinary things beautiful. • Makerspace sign to encourage wrapping and/or weaving ("What can you imagine making with these fiber arts materials?")
Main Material	• Yarn of different textures and widths • Shoestrings for lacing opportunities with paper
Loose Parts	• Sticks or branches for children to wrap • If you want to give children the opportunity to embellish their designs, provide large beads with large openings. • If you want to begin with lacing, provide paper and watercolors for children to make and embellish their own lacing boards.
Tools and Attachments	• Scissors • String for threading beads and attaching them to the sticks and branches • Hole punch for children to make their own holes to lace

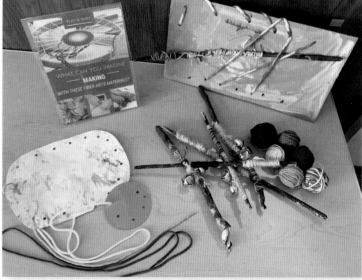

Before and after of the transformation from lacing area to emerging fiber arts makerspace

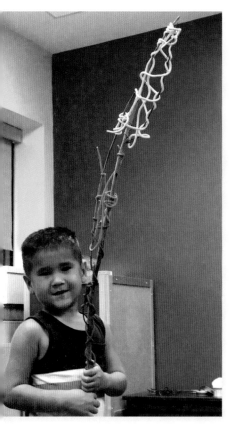

Jansen wraps a tree branch and shares that he made a sunset.

A child weaves with yarn and a cardboard loom.

After giving children time to explore how fiber materials work, use the continuum tool to support the design of future fiber arts makerspaces. Since the possibilities in fiber arts are endless, let's explore four fiber arts categories and then reflect on each to determine its location on the continuum of maker's materials and tools.

The first category we recommend is fiber explorations. This makerspace lets children tinker with a variety of fiber main materials and learn basic techniques. As in the introductory story above, we like to begin with wrapping. Children can consider color and design, but they really focus on the properties of the type of fiber being used. Other techniques in this category include hand knitting and felting.

The next category is weaving. Weaving is using two sets of thread, yarn, or other material to make cloth. All weaving experiences use the same basic motions. We recommend beginning with paper weaving because it is an easy and inexpensive way to introduce children to the over-and-under technique of the weaving process. Once the child has mastered the technique, move on to weaving with different colors, patterns, and fibers and the addition of loose parts.

Next we combine threading, lacing, stitching, and embroidery into one category representing a continuum of stitching skills that develop over time. For example, threading makerspaces allow children to develop fine-motor skills and the concept of threading a needle by stringing loose parts onto a main material such as pipe cleaners or even thread. Children continue to build their fine-motor skills in lacing and are thus introduced to basic hand-sewing skills. Instead of providing commercialized lacing boards, we set up lacing makerspaces where children can create their own shapes, decide where the holes will be punched, and then stitch around the edge with fiber. Next, stitching makerspaces introduce the use of a needle and thread or yarn to embellish or add to a work of art or the medium in which you create your artwork. Finally, embroidery experiences allow children to explore stitching and creating an embellishment.

Our final category is sewing. Sewing is the act of combining two pieces of fabric with needle and thread. One of the first sewing makerspace activities we observed was children sewing their own pincushions with teachers. They learn the basics of tying knots, threading a needle, and troubleshooting throughout a small-scale project. They also develop the concept of making useful things because the pincushion becomes a tool they use each time they sew.

This child is exploring basic stitches to create a character about herself.

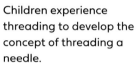

Children experience threading to develop the concept of threading a needle.

Children use their knowledge of stitching to combine two pieces of fabric with needle and thread.

Maker's Continuum of Playing and Making for Fiber Arts

Arts and Crafts

⟵─────────────────────────────────⟶

High Tech

Children experience working with fibers, understanding the textures and ways the material functions by wrapping.	Children develop the concept of over-and-under movements by weaving with paper.	Children weave using fibers and add loose parts to the process.	Children weave using fibers and conductive thread with LEDs.
	Children develop fine-motor skills and are exposed to stitching and sewing tools by threading.	Children develop fine-motor skills and the concept of basic hand-sewing skills by lacing.	Children use a needle and thread/yarn to stitch or to embellish their work of art by stitching and embroidering.	Children use conductive thread, battery packs, and LEDs to sew a circuit.
			Children combine two pieces of fabric with needle and thread by sewing.	

STREAM Learning in the Fiber Arts Makerspace

When children engage in the fiber arts makerspace, they experience powerful STREAM learning that can transfer into other disciplines throughout their lives. Use the prompts below in your fiber arts makerspace to ensure interdisciplinary connections.

Prompts to Ensure STREAM Learning Connections

Science	Makers will do the following: • Incorporate science knowledge by inquiring about the properties of each type of fiber and investigating ways to transform materials into art ("How can you change this material to make what you imagine?")
Technology	• Develop fluency with tools and sewing needles ("How can you use this tool to achieve the stitch or pattern you desire?")
Reading/Literacy	• Verbally share and/or write down the stories they made or information they learned throughout their making, just as folktales and stories have circled around weavers and spinners for centuries ("What stories can you share about who made this art?" "What stories can you imagine while making with fibers?")
Engineering	• Solve the problems they face as engineers and troubleshoot when they make a mistake in their stitching or if the threads become tangled ("What strategies can you use to improve your design?")
Arts	• Design art that holds meaning, pattern, and imagery that unleashes the imagination ("What shapes and designs do you see represented in your piece?")
Mathematics	• Make patterns with fiber materials: "Math is important, because you'll be measuring length, making patterns of odds and evens, working with geometry and shape, and thinking about amounts, such as more, less, and equal" (Carlson 2016, v). ("What patterns can you make using these materials?")

Imagine Making a Fiber Arts Makerspace

The initial purpose of our fiber arts makerspace was to increase makers' curiosity and familiarity with textile materials. Over time the purpose can transition to growing specific skills, such as keeping track of weaving motions to expand children's identities as weavers. When introduced to cardboard looms, children needed to slow down and apply their knowledge of weaving motions. The intent of the following makerspace was for children to experience weaving with yarn of varying textures and thicknesses. They demonstrated their understanding of the materials in selecting the type of yarn and embellishments to incorporate into their artistic designs.

Weaving makerspace with glass loose parts: 1. Inspiration and support (books and sign) 2. Main material (wool yarn) 3. Loose parts (glass beads) 4. Tools and attachments (cardboard loom, needles)

INSPIRATION AND SUPPORT

One afternoon after schools had let out for the day, children from pre-K to fifth grade were invited to attend a fiber arts makerspace at the Clinton Public Library in Clinton, Tennessee. The age range was wide, so we provided a weaving experience that was not too challenging for the younger children, given support with the over-and-under movements, but still engaging for older children. We offered many choices in the color of yarn and also several shapes of looms with which they could make. When the children entered the makerspace, we gathered on the carpet for a read-aloud. The inspiration selected was *Walter's Wonderful Web* by Tim Hopgood. Even though this story is a first book of shapes, it shows the character displaying a growth mindset by persisting, trying new weaving techniques every time his web was not strong enough to withstand the strong winds. Walter wove webs of different shapes and was the perfect inspiration for children to begin imagining what shapes they wanted to weave and what ideas they might share with others in this playing and making experience. We displayed our guiding questions anchor chart to stimulate their making, asking, "What can you imagine making with these weaving materials?" After the lesson the children walked over to the makerspace and began exploring the fiber main materials.

Children drew inspiration from *Walter's Wonderful Web* and reflected on all the shapes they could make.

MAIN MATERIAL

Fiber is the main ingredient in a fiber arts makerspace. It is as necessary to making as flour is to a baker or soil is for a gardener. Consider carefully the type of fiber you would like children to explore and its suitability for wrapping, weaving, threading, lacing, stitching, embroidery, or sewing. In this makerspace we provided chunky wool yarn and thick, solid-colored acrylic yarn to account for the differing fine-motor abilities of the children attending the makerspace. The texture of the finished product will guide you to the fiber choice. For example, ask yourself if you want your project to be silky, soft, scratchy, shiny, or warm, and that will determine the type of fiber you should select.

The most common fibers that we use include the following:

- yarn of varying textures, thicknesses, and colors
- embroidery floss (recommended for stitching, embroidery, and sewing maker-spaces because it comes in a wide variety of colors and can be easily separated if you need a thinner fiber for sewing [Blum and Newman 2017]).
- string
- jute
- thread
- twine
- fabric scraps (Cotton, felt, and fleece tend not to fray as children handle the material.)
- burlap (our favorite fabric to use in embroidery makerspaces because it is inexpensive and has large holes that allow large, blunt needles suitable for young makers to pass through easily)

The children could choose from chunky wool yarn and finer, solid-colored acrylic yarn to make their circle weavings.

Loose parts are incorporated into your fiber arts makerspaces when children are ready to embellish their work. In this weaving makerspace, we supplied a variety of items for children to weave into their designs, including the following:

- glass beads
- pom-poms
- pony beads
- ribbons
- fabric scraps
- nature objects

For threading makerspaces, loose parts such as these help children practice their fine-motor skills:

- plastic and wooden beads
- nature loose parts (leaves, flower petals)

For embellishing in stitching or sewing makerspaces, include the following materials:

- buttons
- sequins
- beads

The children embellish their weavings with glass bead loose parts.

Each fiber arts makerspace requires tools specific to what will be made. For threading, lacing, stitching, embroidery, and sewing makerspaces, you will need the following:

- needles with large eyes (You may begin with plastic and move toward the sharper metal versions.)
- pins to serve as temporary glue
- pincushions
- needle threaders

For weaving makerspaces, the go-to tool is looms. You can make or purchase wood and cardboard looms. You can even make looms out of twigs or craft sticks.

In this makerspace we provided the following items:

- cardboard looms
- fabric scissors
- tape (to hold string to the back of the cardboard)

When fibers are used to attach embellishments, they transform into tools. Therefore, the following are the most common attachments:

- string
- embroidery floss
- yarn
- wire
- tacky glue
- fabric glue
- hot glue

Safety

If you are using metal needles and are afraid of losing track of these pointy tools, include a magnet wand to help children to scoop them up at the end of your time together.

Organization/Aesthetics

Cassie Stephens (2019), author of *Stitch and String Lab for Kids*, recommends creating a sewing kit with the children that includes a pincushion and a sewing book with needle and thread. She also recommends creating a more gender-neutral tackle box to encourage reluctant children.

Spaces for Playing and Making

One morning we attended one of Laurie Kay's sewing makerspaces with a home-school co-op class of four- to seven-year-olds. She chose monsters as inspiration for the children to make because they are gender neutral and come in an unlimited variety of shapes, sizes, colors, and textures. The purpose of her makerspaces is to not only learn sewing skills but also to develop social-emotional skills as children reflect on what they love about themselves and stitch those elements into the characters they make.

Laurie set up the makerspace, arranging a basket of fleece squares in varying shades and patterns, spools of string in bright colors, a bowl of colored eyes, buttons, and a cup containing fabric scissors, needle threaders, and pencils in the middle of each table. Each child had their own bag or sewing kit containing their needles and pins on the pincushion they had made, fabric they had selected

Sewing makerspace where children learn to sew a character they imagine

from their last class, their self-love message, and the project and paper patterns they were currently working on. Six-year-old Truxton looked closely through the collection of different-colored eyes and selected two to place on his character. He tried multiple times to push the eyes through the thick fleece fibers, but he needed more support, so he asked for help from Laurie.

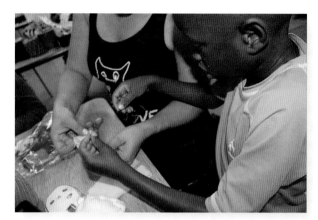

Truxton seeks additional resources to learn how to attach eyes to his character.

Truxton was proud of what he had just learned, and we felt like he was celebrating as he moved his monster around, swinging it high in the air and creating other actions. We asked if he could share what he was doing. "My monster can do splits or walk upside down or jump over many things," he explained, giggling. Just then he expressed that he wanted to name his monster Splitter and that he now needed an orange mouth. Truxton used what he knew about cutting fabric with the fabric scissors to shape the mouth that he imagined.

Truxton then paused to consider the next steps in his making. He concentrated on how to attach the mouth with the stitches he had learned. In doing so he exhibited fluency with his tools and took time to inquire and ask questions of himself on the next steps, all learning practices of the maker movement.

Truxton threads his needle to attach the mouth to his monster.

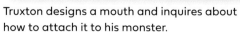

Truxton designs a mouth and inquires about how to attach it to his monster.

Time passed quickly, and each child was proud of what they accomplished that day. They gathered all of their work to show to each other before packing up their sewing kits until the next day. Splitter still needed his orange mouth, but with a quick review of attachment and stitching techniques, Truxton would soon complete a character that displays the attributes he loves about himself: playful, ticklish, and smart!

The children share and celebrate the work they accomplished before leaving for the day.

Documenting Learning in the Fiber Arts Makerspace

Learning Practices that Lead to the Development of a Maker Mindset	Indicators of Learning through Enactment of the Practices
Inquire	• Truxton looked closely at all the eye choices to explore what would work best for his monster.
Tinker	• Truxton took risks and tried multiple ways to push the eyes through the thick material.
Seek and Share Resources	• Truxton recognized that he needed more support and waited patiently for Laurie so he could watch her demonstrate and then learn the technique himself.
Hack and Repurpose	• Truxton returned to the materials to select the orange material for the mouth and used the fabric scissors to make the shape he imagined.
Express Intent	• Truxton named his monster and explained what he looks like.
Develop Fluency	• Truxton demonstrated an increase in his sewing abilities by threading his needle.
Simplify to Complexify	• Truxton demonstrated an understanding of how to sew by carefully considering next steps and attaching the parts to make the face of his emerging monster creation.

More Fiber Arts Makerspaces to Inspire Your Making

In this chapter we have suggested four distinct categories for fiber arts materials and recommended a progression of makerspaces within each category. Below
are some examples to help you imagine more possibilities. Return to this section
throughout the year for more inspiration as your children develop fluency with the
fibers, tools, and other materials that accompany each space.

Threading makerspace with wood
loose parts

Wrapping makerspace with wood loose parts

Ellie threads wooden beads onto a pipe cleaner and imagines making a snake.

Threading makerspace with natural loose parts

Lacing makerspace with paper loose parts

 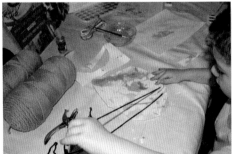 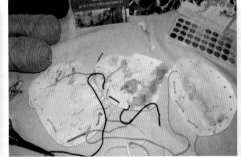

A four-year-old imagines and designs his own lacing card and shares that he made a treehouse.

Weaving makerspace with textile loose parts

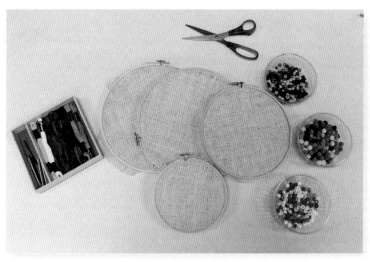

Stitching/embroidery makerspace with plastic loose parts

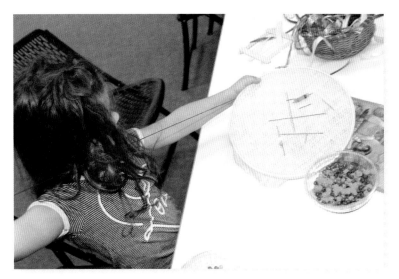

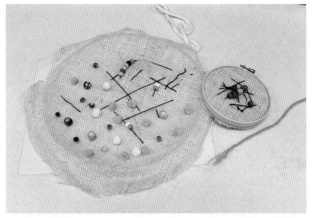

Children explore making marks and embellishing their embroidery.

Sewing makerspace with conductive thread offered at The Muse Knoxville children's museum. The Make Space coordinator assists children in making bracelets that light up.

Making a Mark by becoming socially aware of when someone else is in need of support. We observed an older sister stopping her own embroidery, which she was enjoying, when she saw her little sister becoming frustrated.

Sharing Our Thinking

Educators tend to shy away from the fiber arts makerspace because they feel they lack the necessary skills, especially in progressing across the continuum of materials and tools. We understand: we have felt that way too! All you need is a little inspiration! We have designed the following lesson for creating an embroidery makerspace suggested by a fellow maker, Shannon Merenstein from the Hatch Art Studio. When you provide a few basic materials and tools and allow children time to explore and tinker, beautiful creations emerge. This lesson demonstrates how simple and creative an embroidery makerspace can be when children are free to experiment and create any stitches they imagine. You and your children can't go wrong!

FIBER ARTS MAKERSPACE FOCUS LESSON

Objective: Children will explore stitching techniques by using a needle and yarn to make marks on burlap.

MATERIALS

- types of stitches anchor chart
- *Walter's Wonderful Web* by Tim Hopgood
- small to medium embroidery hoops with burlap stretched inside
- plastic large-eye sewing needles (one for each child)
- yarn of different colors, sizes, and textures (cut pieces ahead of your lesson, one for each child)
- pony beads with holes large enough to fit the needle through the opening
- camera for documentation

Focus and Explore

Connect: *"We have been exploring the textures of yarn and discovering many ways to use and make things with this fabric. Today I would like to show you another type of fiber arts where you can use the same material, yarn, to make stitches on fabric. So we will explore stitching techniques by using a needle and yarn to make marks on burlap fabric."*

Teach: *"Before we delve right into the different marks we can make with our new tools, I thought it might be fun to read a story about a spider who makes many different types of shapes with his thread. He has some bumps along the way, but he doesn't give up and continues to try new ways to make his web."* Read *Walter's Wonderful Web* and highlight the different shapes he makes with his stitching material. Focus on how it is important to explore all different kinds of shapes because it will make you a strong maker, weaver, and sewer in the end. *"Wow, Walter sure did make a lot of beautiful shapes or marks, even though most of them were a little wobbly. I would* *like to share with you some marks you can explore making on burlap in an embroidery hoop."* Show children the types of stitches chart to help them imagine what marks they can make or stitch. Hold up the preassembled embroidery hoop with burlap. *"Today you will begin to explore stitching. Stitching is the act of using a needle and thread or yarn to embellish or add to your work of art. The first step is to get our stitching tools ready."* Demonstrate threading the needle and making a large knot.

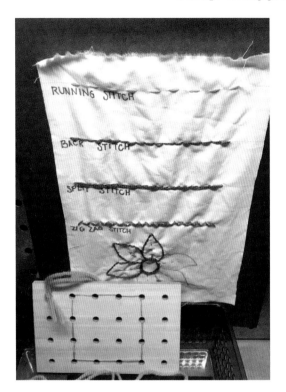

Stitching techniques anchor chart displayed at The Muse

Active Involvement: *"Now I want you to try getting your needle ready to stitch. Don't worry! Just like Walter, we will get this, and I am here to support and help you along the way."* Allow children to select a piece of precut yarn and practice threading it and tying a big knot so it doesn't slip through the burlap.

Imagine

"Now you are ready to begin making marks on your fabric. Remember, there is no wrong way to make and stitch your art. You may stitch marks from our chart or create your own. The important thing is to persist like Walter if you get stuck, and have fun!" Ask children to pause and think about what mark they are imagining on their fabric. Record their ideas on the Class at a Glance form (see appendix C).

Play and Make

Facilitate starting from the back of the hoop and pulling the needle through and then back down again. Using the Learning Practices Documentation form (see appendix B), document the learning practices children exhibit by highlighting the behaviors you observed and making notes on what they say and do. For example, look for children taking risks with their stitches and pausing to evaluate the next steps in their process as evidence of tinkering behaviors.

Share

Consider asking a child who displayed frustration while stitching but continued to persist, just like Walter from the book, to share a maker talk. Prompt the child to explain to the group the difficulties they faced. Encourage all the children not to give up. Take a few minutes to brainstorm strategies (take a deep breath, retrace your stitches, ask a friend, wait patiently for a teacher).

Children make marks and explore stitching for the first time.

In the fiber arts makerspace, we have used children's books to inspire work with textiles and also develop a curiosity around these materials. Books we have used in our fiber arts makerspaces include the following:

Extra Yarn by Marc Barnett

The Goat in the Rug by Charles L. Blood

Knit Together by Angela Dominguez

A Hat for Mrs. Goldman: A Story about Knitting and Love by Michelle Edwards

Woolbur by Leslie Helakoski

Walter's Wonderful Web by Tim Hopgood

Weaving the Rainbow by George Ella Lyon

Rainbow Weaver by Linda Elovitz Marshall

Cloth Lullaby: The Woven Life of Louise Bourgeois by Amy Novesky

Twig by Aura Parker

One Plastic Bag by Miranda Paul

Knitting Nell by Julie Jersild Roth

The Weaver by Qian Shi

Sophie's Masterpiece by Eileen Spinelli

The Kindness Quilt by Nancy Elizabeth Wallace

Next Steps in Transforming Spaces

Creating a fiber arts makerspace may feel uncomfortable because many of us lack the sewing skills that we automatically assume are required to share these materials with children. We have felt that way, but once we witnessed children exploring fibers and showing such kindness to themselves and the ones they love through their making, we knew that this was a makerspace we had to pursue. We now challenge you to explore along with the children and use the maker's continuum to progress through making experiences as you develop proficiency and knowledge in the fibers, techniques, and tools. Observe and celebrate as children tinker and take risks with their weaving and stitching attempts, and highlight children seeking and sharing resources by collaborating with each other to solve problems. Then shift your focus to how they are growing in their maker identities as weavers and sewers through aspects of the maker mindset. Take a moment to have a maker talk with your colleagues and reflect on how your children are developing in their maker mindsets as well as your next steps in this fiber arts journey.

- What learning practices have you observed children displaying as they wrap, weave, lace, stitch, or sew? How are these behaviors connected to the maker mindset?
- What strategies or systems can you put in place to encourage collaboration and persistence when children face frustration?
- What inspiration will you choose to create excitement for making with fibers?
- What is your plan for transforming or adding this space to your STEAM learning areas?

HOW WOULD YOU LIKE TO

SHARE

YOUR IDEAS WITH OTHERS?

An invitation for children to share their stories, ideas, thoughts, and opinions with others

CHAPTER 9

Maker Talks

I sketch and write to capture my play.
My stories live here at the end of the day.
Eager to share for all to learn and enjoy,
We make, share, and celebrate—this brings us great joy!

Stories to Inspire Making

The children, ages four to eight, gathered their materials—bits of felt, heaps of wool, and lengths of string, all assembled on felt canvases—and brought them to the meeting area to prepare for the maker talk one afternoon at a pop-up makerspace at the local library. Each child carefully laid the collage masterpieces on the floor or in their laps, as if protecting a great treasure. These valid and artistic creations held ideas, memories, and stories that they were eager to share. Each textile had been carefully selected, rearranged, and positioned in the perfect place to communicate their thinking. Sally Petal, age four, climbed into the maker's chair first and began describing how she made her character. She pointed to the character's head and arms and told everyone how her character was feeling unhappy.

Adaptations for the Youngest Makers

When young children are showing you what they made, help them build language skills during a maker talk. Restate what you saw them build or what you observed them pretending during their play and ask follow-up questions. Using the example from our story, you could say, "So you made a girl who is feeling unhappy. What kinds of things could she do to help herself feel better? Let's name some things she could do to solve this problem in the story you are beginning to play and make." Then list action words that will develop vocabulary and inspire additional details when making.

Next, Caspian, age eight, wanted to show how he made a face just like the artist did in the book provided in the makerspace. He stayed on the floor and invited the children over to watch him work. He demonstrated how he cut small pieces of yarn to form the shape of the face and explained that he was still working on adding more details with the materials.

Finally, one of the children asked Cole, age four, what he had made with the materials. "I made a brown bear, and he fell off the bike and hurt his ankle. Then he bandaged it, and he took off and was better." We wanted to know where the bandage was in his collage, and Cole pointed to the yellow ribbon he had laid across the heap of brown fur representing his bear. The children were excited to see one another's creations and passed their work around to see the details. After each maker shared their ideas, they selected a cheer to celebrate the playing and making they had shared. The room filled with booming rounds of applause as a smile lit up each

Children sharing their ideas, stories, and processes with fellow makers after a session of making at a pop-up makerspace at the Clinton Public Library

child's face. They had come. They had made. They had shared. And they had been celebrated. These accomplishments are central to developing a culture of makers willing to collaborate and share.

Why Are Maker Talks Important to Introduce to Children?

When artists, engineers, sculptors, inventors, sewers, and other makers imagine new ideas and perfect their skills as they play and make, they are often in the sanctuary of their own studios or makerspaces. These are safe places, full of inspiration and support, where they keep all the materials, loose parts, and tools needed to hack and repurpose their ideas. Makers begin with an idea, but only as they spend time inquiring and testing out ideas with the material they have chosen to explore do they truly discover the potential of their work. The chapters leading up to this have shown you many ways to establish, transform, and grow makerspaces where children learn to explore, take risks, and develop fluency with tools over time.

However, after the professional artist is satisfied with their work, they step out of the studio and share their work with the world. They may display their work in a gallery, invite the public into their studio, exhibit at local fairs, or use their work to teach techniques in local schools and community centers. In the maker's world, sharing happens not just at the end of a project or experience but throughout the process, so the maker gains knowledge and support from other makers. Through makerspace experiences, we want our children to develop the maker mindset to share and collaborate with others. "Through exchanging ideas, helping one another succeed, and celebrating both successes and challenges, a culture of collaboration and sharing is cultivated" (Regalla 2016, 265). This is an important goal of our maker talks.

Another goal is to teach children to embrace mistakes and shift their perspective to see difficulties as an opportunity to seek and share resources. When children share the troubles they experienced during making with their community, they demonstrate an understanding that we all need to persist and improve our practices to accomplish our goals—a growth mindset. Their brave sharing of these situations will not only bring the maker community together for support but also help other future makers who encounter a similar problem. "They learn that ideas are valued and important whether right or wrong, that people may have different ideas, and that one can learn by asking questions of others" (Chalufour and Worth 2004, 5). Maker talks are a crucial part of our makerspaces, and we recommend that educators provide time and structure to foster these conversations in their STREAM learning environments.

Remaking a Sharing Time to Maker Talks

When early childhood educators provide time for children to play, or when STEAM educators teach for a specific class time, best practice is to summarize the learning in some way before moving on for the day. Consider repurposing this time of reflection as a space for children to share and collaborate in a maker talk. A maker talk is "when a few children are selected or volunteer to share how they made their story with their friends" (Compton and Thompson 2018, 70). It also applies to sharing ideas, projects, information, and strategies with fellow makers. Start slowly with five-minute talks, and gradually increase the time of sharing as stamina increases. Offer one or two simple questions to prompt their sharing. Here is a sample plan to introduce maker talks into your day.

Designing Your First Maker Talk

Inspiration and Support	• Whatever the children make is the inspiration for all! Take a photo and print or project it to help the child reflect on what they made. • Provide support by asking questions about what they made. ("Can you point to the parts of your piece?" "Can you tell us what this [indicate a specific part] is?")
Main Area	• Create a special place of importance where sharing happens (designated chair, front carpet spot).
Tools	• Visuals help children to communicate their thinking. Take and share photos from a camera, computer, or tablet. This gives the child a visual to refer to and helps others visualize as well. Start with whatever you have access to right now.

After giving a child a few minutes to answer your prompts or fully describe what they made, model for the other children that a way to respond to a presentation is by asking a question. Start by asking, "What do you want to do next with this project?" Then begin to build routines of celebrating each other by learning different cheers. After you have established a maker talk routine, use the continuum tool to keep their conversations and collaborations growing throughout the year.

Maker's Continuum of Sharing and Collaborating

Arts and Crafts

High Tech

SHARING

Children use a picture or the work itself to • explain what they made; • demonstrate how they made their piece; and • explain next steps in their making.	Children bring materials to the meeting area or display images of their work in process to • share successes or a strategy they discovered while playing and making that could help their maker community; and • share the process of what they made over time and what meaning it holds for them.	Children present their work digitally to • explain what connections they made while making and share any successes with processes, materials, or tools; and • share struggles or difficulties they are having while trying to make an imagined idea.

COLLABORATING

Children learn to give feedback by asking questions such as these: • "What is this in your piece?" • "What is happening?" • "What do you want to do with your project?"	Children learn how to give compliments by referring back to the child's artifact: • "I like this part of your piece because . . ."	Children learn how to offer advice. This might involve researching possible solutions digitally and presenting the research found in the maker talk: • "I think you might want to try . . ." Children receiving the advice learn how to respond by saying the following: • "I'll think about it." • "No thank you, but thanks for trying to help." • "That's a good idea, thank you!"

STREAM Learning in Maker Talks

When children have time to share, reflect, and collaborate with each other on solving problems, you are promoting STREAM connections to learning. Use the ideas below during your maker talks to promote connections across disciplines.

Prompts to Ensure STREAM Learning Connections

Science	Makers will: • Use their five senses to closely observe the details of what their fellow maker has made and shared ("How has this maker used the materials to make what they imagined?")
Technology	• Use technology tools (stop-action, green screen, robotic blocks) in their making to represent an idea ("How did this maker communicate their idea? How could you use this technology when you are playing and making?")
Reading/Literacy	• Develop communication skills when explaining what they made, and talk in a story structure or provide information to share • Publish stories or information on paper as writers ("What stories/information can you share about what you made?")
Engineering	• Share new ways of making that solve a problem that a maker encountered ("What problems did you encounter while making? How did you discover a new way of making to solve your problem?")
Arts	• Use their knowledge of the elements of art to describe what they made ("What have you learned about being an artist that helped you make this piece of work?")
Mathematics	• Use mathematical tools to help them in their playing and making ("How did you use math skills in your making to accomplish your goal?")

Imagine Engaging Children in Maker Talks

The purpose of maker talks is to provide time for children to share, feel proud, gain confidence, seek advice, and know that what they say matters in their maker community and beyond. Children may volunteer or be asked to talk by the educator if they have displayed a specific skill, learning practice, or direct connection to the focus lesson of the day to help reinforce the teaching point for all children in the learning environment.

INSPIRATION AND SUPPORT

The children's creations are the real and authentic inspiration and support to all makers in your STREAM learning spaces. Keep a record of what your children have made, not only to support them in communicating during a maker talk, but also to post throughout the makerspaces as inspiration for others who are having difficulties imagining ideas. The materials that the child used to make their piece also serve as supports. For example, if the child made a sculpture with playdough, ask the child to bring the sculpture and the tools to demonstrate how they added texture or other design elements while making. As always, books can be both inspiration and support in the makerspace; see the list at the end of this chapter for books that help children understand what it means to support each other when sharing our work.

Children can also sign up and volunteer to communicate at the end of the class. This gives children an opportunity to request support if they have problems in making or need advice or expertise from the rest of their maker community. When they are proud of something they made, this is also a chance to share it and celebrate with their peers. Of course, more children will want to share than we have time for each day; establish a routine of asking children to turn and talk with a peer before moving on for the day. This allows each child to be celebrated and have their voice heard, ensuring that they feel valued.

After hosting countless whole-group maker talks in classrooms, libraries, and museum settings, we have identified seven components to help with your own maker talks with children. Remember to start slow and gradually increase the time as the children's stamina increases and new conversation starters are added to their discussion repertoire.

Main Components of Maker Talks

- Gather all materials and tools prior to the maker talk.
- Explain what you are making and how you are making.
- Share success and lessons learned.
- Share difficulties and seek advice.

- Tell about any connections this made you think of as you were making (Did it remind you of a memory, idea, or information you learned?).
- Share your thinking about what you plan to do next.
- Open up the discussion to ask questions, receive compliments, and request advice from your maker community.

GATHER ALL MATERIALS AND TOOLS PRIOR TO THE MAKER TALK

When it is a child's turn to speak, have them gather all of their making materials and bring them to the meeting area. If children are working with large-scale projects, such as blocks or a fragile piece of art, take pictures and print or project them to help the child communicate what they are making. The group can also join the child at a large piece for the maker talk. Support young children by providing prompts, such as, "This is a picture of what you have been making. Can you tell us about what you made? Can you point to the parts of your construction (or sculpture, collage, and so on) and tell us what you did?"

EXPLAIN WHAT YOU ARE MAKING AND HOW YOU ARE MAKING

We want to emphasize student-led conversations, so we suggest teaching children some ways to begin engaging discussions by considering relevant questions. For example, ask, "What are you making?" Have the child explain what they are making. Request specific details on how they are constructing, sculpting, weaving, and so forth. Just as we encourage readers to point to the pages of a book and provide text evidence to support their thinking, we encourage children to use the materials they are making as they explain. In a maker talk, we want children to focus on how they are making by demonstrating ways they attached objects or explaining what tools they used during the making process. Children can engage in maker talks one-on-one with an adult, in a small group setting, or during a whole-group share.

Sharing his thinking and his planning one-on-one with an adult.

Sharing in a small group using the materials to show what she was making

Sharing with the whole class using documentation to discuss questions, compliment, and seek advice from their maker community

Celebrate successes during reflection. Children should ponder, "Do you have any successes to share with your fellow makers?" or "Did you learn any lessons today while you were making?" Sometimes children feel shy about sharing what has gone right in their making experiences. With practice, modeling, and prompting, as children reflect on what they learned during their making, they will discover a big idea or an aha moment that could help develop fluency in another maker. "Remember that aha moments do not need to be completely revolutionary, never-before-thought-of ideas; they just have to be ideas that lead your students or your classroom community to see things a little differently" (Mraz and Hertz 2015, 148). These last two conversation starters are when children begin to shift their maker talks from just explaining or rehashing what they have done to truly reflecting on what we can all learn as makers!

Portor is sharing a story about an elephant flying a plane that begins to break down. His eyes light up, and he says, "Now I need to make my plane sound like it's breaking down!" He adds metal loose parts to the back and encloses it with fabric. Now when he rehearses his story and shakes his construction, the sound of the metal parts matches what he imagined. Aha moments include the realization that when you share what you are making, you might have another idea to add to your project.

SHARE DIFFICULTIES AND SEEK ADVICE

Another set of questions for children to consider is, "Are you having any trouble in your makerspace?" The conversations that follow promote a growth mindset by supporting children's need to embrace mistakes and celebrate their achievements. Children and adults can feel vulnerable when things go wrong or when they think they have failed. The key is to develop the habit of reaching out for help or seeking additional resources. One way to begin this conversation is to have children identify the problem and then seek advice from other makers. When children share with others who might have had a similar experience when making, they will be better able to silence negative self-talk and focus on the positive work of reflection. "Creating a space for collective, community reflection helps maintain a balance between thinking through what went wrong and thinking about how things will go better the next time" (Mraz and Hertz 2015, 142).

TELL ABOUT ANY CONNECTIONS THIS MADE YOU THINK OF AS YOU WERE MAKING

The next conversation starter stems from the research gathered for our first book, *StoryMaking*. Allow children time to make connections to what they are making and ponder, "What stories or books can you imagine by making with these materials?" Many times children narrate as they play and make and go back to imagine characters or settings that they weave into their making. Rich oral storytelling experiences can occur during maker talks, and they support children's oral development. We write like we talk, so "writing in the air" opportunities help children understand the ways stories are told and prepare them to share their making experiences on paper as another form of communication.

 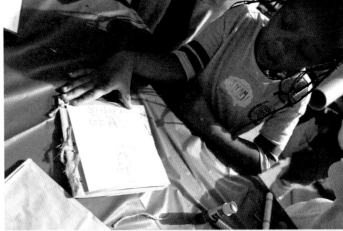

Naraye makes a tent with a campfire at the Global Cardboard Challenge at The Muse Knoxville. After playing and making, she is inspired to share by writing a story about a family camping trip.

Narratives are not the only genre of storytelling and writing that children may engage in while they are making. Children may know a lot of information about a specific topic and incorporate that knowledge into their making. They may also have strong opinions that come to the surface during maker's talks. Therefore, it is important to generalize conversation starters so children know that any genre of writing is celebrated. When stories, information, or opinions surface in the makerspaces or during a maker talk, highlight what the child is doing by labeling the type of "writing in the air" that was shared, and support the child by providing more details to support their oral language growth.

SHARE YOUR THINKING ABOUT WHAT YOU PLAN TO DO NEXT

The final conversation starter for children to consider is sharing what they plan to do next in their making. For example, if the child encountered problems, how will they persist and continue their making tomorrow? If they are feeling successful with what they are making, how do they plan to continue their work? For children making stories or explaining information in their work, do they want to try repurposing some of their ideas and remaking them in another makerspace to see if new details surface? When you wrap up maker talks with this type of discussion, you are modeling the learning practice of expressing intention. Children will develop this habit of reflecting and making next steps in their pursuit of their goals.

Isabella shares her plan to return to the pop-up makerspace next week to continue making her penguin with blocks. As she remakes her idea using a different material, embroidery, she shares a new detail in her story.

OPEN UP THE DISCUSSION TO ASK QUESTIONS, RECEIVE COMPLIMENTS, AND REQUEST ADVICE FROM YOUR MAKER COMMUNITY

Finally, include an opportunity for children to support one another's making. We first teach children how to ask questions about what the child just shared. Model pointing to the work or photos and asking, "What is this part of your project?" or "What do you want to do next in the makerspace?" Later show children how to give compliments by providing them the language frame: "I like the part . . ." Provide an example of how children can give advice to each other. Additional language frames, such as "I think you should . . ." or "Have you thought about . . ." model respectful feedback (Compton and Thompson 2018). The book *Thanks for the Feedback (I Think!)* by Julia Cook is an excellent inspiration to help children develop a growth mindset and learn ways to understand and accept compliments and feedback.

Celebrating!

Sharing with Museum Walks

Another way to share with other makers is through museum walks. This sharing format allows children to display the day's work. It helps makers notice details, share insights, and reflect on one another's making experiences. Arrange these museum walks for viewing the work of everyone in the class or select a specific makerspace to visit. Museum walks can occur once a week so you and the children, and even families, can see the progress of every maker in your space. As you visit each makerspace on your walk, invite the children to talk about what they have been playing and making in this space. Then bring in the language of discussing the details of art from chapter 2, asking children to describe what they see in the work displayed. Chalufour and Worth (2003) provide some suggested follow-up questions for sharing in this format, and we have generalized them to fit our maker talks. Use your documentation notes to ask follow-up questions that focus on making strategies and designs. For example, you might say the following:

- I noticed that when you were attaching this piece to your cardboard structure, it kept falling. How did you get it to stay attached this time?

- Can you show us how you made these textures in your clay? What tool and technique did you use?
- How were you able to make that color to include in your piece of art?
- Can you explain what shapes you used in your collage and what they represent?

Museum walk

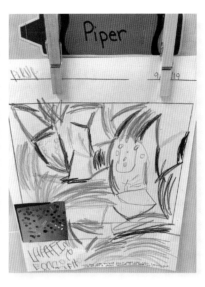

Piper shares details of her art on display during a museum walk and describes how she improved her design as she remade her collage into a drawing.

Another way to share and celebrate children's work is to display photo documentation.

Sharing by Using Other "Languages" in Maker Talks

What a child is making with others can be shared in the other Hundred Languages as well. We often teach children who are learning English for the first time or who have communication needs. We also have children who are building confidence and children who have preferences or talents for particular modes of communicating and sharing. We include as many communication methods as possible so all children have the freedom to express their ideas and develop fluency with other styles, methods, and tools. Here are a few examples of other forms of sharing:

- Children can display their work (with a written artist statement, just as professional artists display their work in a gallery exhibit).

Children's work from the Kinderoo Children's Academy in Ocala, Florida, is displayed for the school community along with a statement of what their art represents.

- Children can gather props, costumes, or sets and act out their work to communicate by demonstrating or acting out what they made, or they can use an app such as Green Screen by DoInk to create a production.
- Children can design instruments, select music—or even make music with programs like Scratch—and perform a dance to communicate characters, feelings, or information from their making projects.
- Children can use technology to share their making with an audience (stop-motion animation, digital drawings, photos on tablet) (Compton and Thompson 2018).

Playing and Making Spaces for Sharing

Over a few days, Cai and Cole, ages two and four, were playing and making in a performance makerspace that was set up in their home. One of the boys had used Mylar, tape, and metal loose parts to create an astronaut suit along with a prop that explained a Taco Planet story he had imagined, played, and made. Now he was eager to share, but he didn't want just to explain what he had done. Cole wanted to put his ideas in action and show his family how he had made a show for us to enjoy.

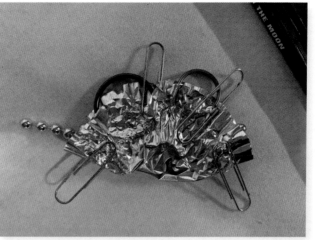

A space helmet made by creating a circlular hole for the boy's face and using the metal loose parts to make a taco prop to match the story he wanted to share

Cole searched for a new way for him to share his making and discovered the high-tech Green Screen app by DoInk. A quick trip to the local store to buy a ninety-seven-cent green tablecloth and he was ready for his performance.

Cole wondered how he could make his movie as he watched the instructions showing how to put one together. The first step was to imagine what image he wanted as his background to represent the setting of his story. He explored the pages of the books from his makerspace, seeking the just-right picture to help him share. He selected a picture of the surface of the moon with a satellite, or, as he called it, a "rocket." He said, "I want this one because this is what Taco Planet looks like, and this is my rocket blasting off in space." It was now time to get dressed. He gathered his materials and asked for assistance in making his costume stay on his head while he acted out and performed his story. When he was ready, he stood in front of the green tablecloth, prop in his hand, and began sharing and acting out his story. He spent time exploring and acting out parts of his story and then calling out, "Stop!" so he could watch how it looked. Then he said that he was ready to tell his story and called out, "Action! Once upon a time, I go to a Taco Planet in my space rocket. And I ate all the tacos. I stayed there with my alien friends. And the end."

This was a new and exciting way for him to share his making with others. During a maker talk, Cole shared the video he had made collaboratively with his parent and proudly showed everyone how they could use this new technology too!

The young maker prepares to create his movie to share in an upcoming maker talk.

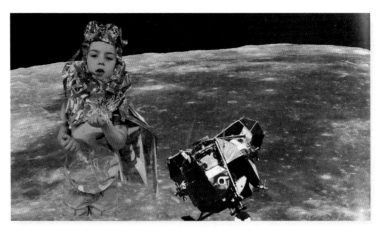

A screenshot of what his movie looks like using the Green Screen app by DoInk

Children not only grow as storytellers and presenters as they share, but they also continue to display the behaviors of the learning practices during maker talks. Here are a few examples from our documentation story to highlight how learning continues from makerspaces to maker talks.

Documenting Learning in a Maker Talk

Learning Practices that Lead to the Development of a Maker Mindset	Indicators of Learning through Enactment of the Practices
Inquire	• Cole showed curiosity when he wondered how he could best show an audience what he had made.
Tinker	• Cole played and tested acting out different actions to see what it looked like on the video recording.
Seek and Share Resources	• Cole asked for assistance in getting his materials ready for sharing.
Hack and Repurpose	• After watching the different versions of his actions, Cole reflected on what he liked best and incorporated those ideas into his final version.
Express Intent	• Cole clearly stated that he wanted to make a movie to share about his Taco Planet story.
Develop Fluency	• After many attempts to press Play to record, Cole understood how the technology worked to share his story.
Simplify to Complexify	• Cole combined his use of materials from the makerspace and technology to share to make something meaningful to him and his family.

Children can communicate what they have made, what they have learned, and what stories and information they have created in so many ways. Here are a few ideas to inspire transforming and sustaining excitement in your maker talks over time.

More Sharing Spaces to Inspire Your Maker Talks

Use these images of our wide variety of maker talks to help you imagine and plan ways for your children to share their important work and knowledge with others.

Sharing by presenting in front of an audience

Sharing by displaying work

Children participate in collaborative sharing in a group or individually share by performing with props and even wearing their art.

Sharing by playing digital stories

Sharing by dancing with music, Alice threaded a string with beads and made up a dance with it.

Making a Mark by sharing and taking action. Students in Ms. Willis's first-grade classroom at Phillippi Shores Elementary in Sarasota make signs to demonstrate their knowledge of how erosion can affect their own environments.

Sharing Our Thinking

It takes time for children to develop conversation skills, just as it does to learn to work with a specific material or tool in a makerspace. Therefore, the lesson provided below is generative and can be used at different times to add another conversation starter to their skill set. Create an anchor chart called "How to Share What We Are Making," and add a new way to share each time you teach this focus lesson on improving maker talks.

MAKER TALKS FOCUS LESSON

Objective: Children will learn ways to talk with each other by looking at our projects and sharing our experiences in maker talks.

MATERIALS
- *Louise Loves Art* by Kelly Light
- child's product from a selected makerspace for the focus lesson
- enlarged photo of another child's work for the focus lesson
- photo documentation or actual piece of each child's making

- anchor chart titled "How to Share What We Are Making"
- marker
- documentation notes on what children have been making

Focus and Explore

Connect: *"Yesterday I was rereading one of our favorite books,* Louise Loves Art, *and it made me think about how all of you are using the materials in each maker-space to express your imagination on the outside. Then I got to the page where she is gathering up all of her art and displaying it throughout the house, and the work she was most proud of making went on display on the fridge for others to see. This got me thinking! We need to find a common time and space for us to share what we are making with each other just like Louise did with her brother Art. Today we will learn ways to talk with each other by looking at our projects and sharing our experiences in maker talks."*

Teach: Select a piece of work that a child has been making from any makerspace. *"Today I was watching (name) select pieces of paper to put on her collage and then remove some and get a different material instead. (Name), can you show us what you did? Why did you decide to select a different material to make the picture you were imagining?"* Provide time for the child to point to her collage or other makerspace work selected and describe what she was making.

This time, project or show an enlarged photo of a child's work from any maker-space. *"I noticed that (name) was building a very tall structure out of our wooden blocks. Can you tell us about what you are building? How did you keep it from falling?"*

Turn to the anchor chart and write, "Share what you are making and how you made it." *"Makers, we just discovered a new way to share our making with one another. We can bring our materials or photos to our meeting area and explain how we are making our projects. I'm excited for you all to share your imagination with each other during this maker talk time."*

Active Involvement: *"Now that you've seen a few examples of how to talk about what you are making, I would like you to turn and talk to your shoulder partner and give it a try. Explain what you made and how you are making it as well."* You can have a child practice from a picture taken that day or the day before, or allow the child to take the peer to the makerspace to view the work. Since children are not leaving the meeting space to go off and play and make, you will have the opportunity to listen in and observe any learning practices as the partners practice how to share. For example, if you see a child sharing how they made their piece, they are sharing their expertise and demonstrating the learning practice of "seek and share resources."

Share

"Today we learned a new way to talk with each other by looking at our projects and sharing our experiences in maker talks. When we are sharing, we can describe what we are making and explain how we are making our work. I can't wait for you all to share your hard work and creative imaginations each day during our maker talks."

SUGGESTED BOOKS TO INSPIRE MAKERS TO SHARE AND COLLABORATE

Throughout the book we have used children's literature to inspire children making in specific makerspaces. Books also provide a strong message of how we can best share our making with each other. Below are some books we have used in our maker talks:

Thanks for the Feedback (I Think!) by Julia Cook
The Rabbit Listened by Cori Doerrfeld
Louise and Andie: The Art of Friendship by Kelly Light
Louise Loves Art by Kelly Light
The Invisible Boy by Trudy Ludwig

Next Steps in Transforming Sharing Time to Maker Talks

No matter the questions you choose for your children to ponder or the components that you select for children to share for the day, provide time to share in a maker talk. All too often we are rushed by the clock and this important aspect of a maker community is cut. This sharing space is too important to our children's lives as budding makers, artists, engineers, sculptors, inventors, and weavers to leave out. Support the development of their maker mindsets in the early years so they can learn valuable lessons of troubleshooting, persisting, taking pride in their work, and finding support in a community of like-minded peers. Take a moment to have a maker talk with your colleagues and reflect on how your children are developing a maker mindset. Collaborate to consider next steps in your transformation of sharing time.

- Think of a time when a child had a powerful conversation about what they made. What made this talk so powerful? What learning practices did you observe that made it so?
- How will you ensure that time for sharing in a maker talk is protected so all children have an opportunity to share throughout the week? What strategies or routines do you need to put in place to make this happen?
- Ask your children, "What new skills have you learned in sharing your work with others?" Reflect on how this is connected to the maker mindset.

Conclusion

Yay! You've made it to the end! We want to celebrate with you and thank you for joining us on this journey. We cannot wait to see all the innovative and wonderful makerspaces you design and set up. We want to hear about your enactment of the learning practices as you wonder and think about inspirations and materials (inquire); set goals, big and small, for yourself (express intent); play around and try out ideas and materials (tinker); check in with your colleagues for advice and ideas (seek and share resources); change your minds, try again, revise, and modify (hack and repurpose); develop routines and processes that grow your children's mindsets (develop fluency); use simple inspirations and materials to enable your children to make their complex thinking visible (simplify to complexify); and collaborate and share along the way with your colleagues and with us! You are a maker, and by enacting the learning practices of the maker movement, you are growing your own maker mindset as well as those of your early learners.

Our overarching goal has been to inspire and support you as you design and set up makerspaces where children can enact the learning practices of the maker movement to grow their maker mindsets. Consider your own mindset as you have a maker talk with your colleagues:

- What surprised you the most as you transformed your areas to makerspaces? What do you think your biggest aha moment has been as you transformed your areas to makerspaces? (Makers exhibit a sense of wonder.)
- What have you noticed about your children as they've engaged in your makerspaces? What materials do they like the most? Which makerspaces are their favorites? How long are they engaged? (Makers are mindful observers.)
- Have you noticed children crossing boundaries of spaces, moving materials and ideas from space to space? In what STREAM learning areas have you noticed the most improvement and growth? Have your students surprised you with their innovations? (Makers are STREAM innovators.)
- How has your confidence grown as you've transformed your spaces? Consider your accomplishments and celebrate your progress! (Makers develop social-emotional efficacy.)

- Congratulations on your perseverance! Have you overcome frustrations? What did you do to figure out solutions to problems along the way? What strategies did you use to keep moving forward? (Makers enact a growth mindset.)
- Share with your colleagues about your plans for next steps. Celebrate your growth! You are a maker and have built your own maker mindset! (Makers share and collaborate.)

We are so looking forward to hearing from you about your early learners' stories, projects, and thinking as they imagine, play, make, and share. Please keep us posted! Don't forget to upload your pictures and comments to www.storymakers.us.

Appendices

Appendix A: Letter to Families

Dear Families,

Your children are makers! They are using loose parts, found materials, and recyclables to imagine, play, make, and share amazing stories, ideas, thinking, and projects. They are learning through play. We are going to set up some makerspaces in our classroom. A makerspace is a place where children use developmentally appropriate open-ended materials, loose parts, and tools to imagine, play, make, and share their ideas, projects, stories, or thinking.

We would like your help in collecting materials for our makerspaces. All the materials you collect should fit into the attached paper bag. Please don't go out and buy anything. Instead, we would like bits and pieces that you already have at home. We hope you will look through your junk drawer, go on a nature walk in your neighborhood, or recycle items from a sewing kit or a toolbox. The goal is to repurpose items you may already have at home.

Please keep safety in mind! We cannot use sharp, toxic, or potentially harmful materials. These are some ideas of materials our children would love to use in their playing and making:

Nature	Wood	Paper / Cardboard	Plastic	Metal / Reflective	Textiles (Fabric)
acorns	clothespins	cardboard	acetate shapes	air ducts	beanbags
bark	corks	mailing	bag clips	aluminum	blankets
clam shells	golf tees	tubes	balloons	canning jar	burlap
coconut	matchsticks	envelopes	beverage caps	lids	cotton balls
shells	palettes	magazines	bingo chips	aluminum foil	doilies
driftwood	wood chips	manila	buttons	binder rings/	embroidery
feathers	wood cookies	folders	CD cases	clips	thread/
flower petals	wood craft	newspaper	cellophane	bottle caps	string
flowers	sticks	old cards	coffee pods		fabric strips
(seasonal)	wood doll pins	paper egg	color paddles		felt
helicopter		cartons	curtain rings		flannel
pods					lace

We can't wait to share, organize, and categorize the materials and use them in our makerspaces. I'll be sending lots of pictures! Thank you for your help.

Appendix B: Learning Practices Documentation Form

LEARNING PRACTICE(S)	**How to Develop a Maker Mindset** WHAT STUDENT SAYS AND DOES Highlight behaviors that child demonstrated	DATE AND COMMENTS
	Sense of Wonder	
Inquire	• Explores properties of materials using five senses • Asks questions • Approaches new materials with curiosity	
	Mindful Observation **Social-Emotional Efficacy** **STREAM Innovations** **Enactment of a Growth Mindset**	
Tinker	• Arranges and rearranges materials • Changes out one material for another • Tests and takes risks with uses of materials • Evaluates form and function	
Hack and Repurpose	• Uses common materials in new ways • Uses new materials in ways other than those for which they were designed • Modifies or enhances materials for new purposes	
Express Intent	• Selects a space to play and make • Expresses what they want to make • Expresses likes, dislikes, interests • Determines next steps in making	
Develop Fluency	• Practices again and again • Gets faster and better at using a material, tool, or attachment • Develops proficiency in using a material, tool, or attachment	
Simplify to Complexify	• Uses simple materials to make something new or complex • Uses simple steps to make something complex • Uses simple processes to develop complex systems	
	Share and Collaborate	
Seek and Share Resources	• Shares expertise with others • Uses stories, books, and illustrations as resources • Uses friends' projects and expertise as resources • Uses adults' expertise as resources • Uses signs as resources • Uses materials as resources	

Appendix C: Class at a Glance Documentation Form

Class at a Glance Documentation Form

Student Name	Date:	Date:	Date:	Date:	Date:	Date:	Date:

Student Name	Date:	Date:	Date:	Date:	Date:	Date:	Date:

Appendix D: Elements of Art

Specific art elements are developmentally appropriate for introduction to young children through materials, discussions, and study of fine art. The following list of the elements of art serves as our inspiration for intentional planning of an arts makerspace and includes suggestions for inspiring art making with a focus on each of the elements.

COLOR

Children experiment with, discover, and mix colors first. They learn to identify and name colors. Starting with just one or two colors in a project gives the students a chance to explore the colors in depth. There are subtleties in naming the colors, or hues, as well as intensities (brightness or dullness), and shades or tones (lightness or darkness) of colors. Discuss the differences between hues—purple and violet and lavender, for example—and let experiments in color lead to all sorts of questions, wonderings, and curiosities.

Contour drawing
with color

LINE

You can find lines in every piece of artwork, historic and contemporary. There are thin lines, thick lines, curved lines, short lines, long lines. We use fine-tip black Sharpies for our contour drawings, or outlines, as "they cultivate the disposition to see drawing as an expression of an idea" (Pelo 2017, 131). You can introduce vocabulary (*heavy*, *parallel*, *zigzag*), compare length and thickness, and experiment with different types of lines. A good question for this element might be, "What do you notice about the lines in this work of art?" or "How might you use lines as you make art?"

Contour drawing with lines

SHAPE

This goes beyond the identification of specific shapes in artworks. It's an examination of the interplay between shapes that fit together, overlap, strike a balance, have space between them, and exist in isolation. Take note of odd shapes, uneven shapes, cylindrical and geometric shapes—all kinds of shapes. The shapes can be solid, be shadowed, or represent three-dimensional objects. "Drawing pens are best for drawing the shape of something" (Pelo 2017, 134).

Contour drawing with shape

TEXTURE

Texture uses the sense of touch. It's the feel of a surface, or its tactile quality. Children can differentiate between textures, from sticky to bumpy to rough to smooth. The different mediums of art each have different textures, as do the different weights of papers used for drawing, finger painting, watercolor painting, and more. Children naturally love to touch materials in their environments, and since they can't typically touch famous works of art, we can discuss what textures their eyes observe and notice.

SPACE

Space is the distance between the representations in a piece of art. Items may be separated by boundaries, or sometimes they overlap. Space can suggest a feeling (crowded, darkness) or delineate what the artist is communicating or representing. Children can experiment with space by taking time with the placement of their representations, trying out different iterations until they find the one that most closely resembles their thinking.

Contour drawing
with space

Resnick, Mitchel. 2016. "All I Really Need to Know (About Creative Thinking) I Learned (By Studying How Children Learn) in Kindergarten." MIT Media Lab. http://web .media.mit.edu/~mres/papers/kindergarten-learning-approach.pdf.

Resnick, Mitchel, Elyse Eidman-Aadahl, and Dale Dougherty. 2016. "Making–Writing– Coding." In *Makeology: Makers as Learners*, vol. 2, edited by Kylie Peppler, Erica Rosenfeld Halverson, and Yasmin B. Kafai, 229–40. New York: Routledge.

Rucci, Barbara. 2016. *Art Workshop for Children*. Beverly, MA: Quarry Books.

Smith, Sheila Dorothy. 2012. *Sandtray Play and Storymaking: A Hands-on Approach to Build Academic, Social, and Emotional Skills in Mainstream and Special Education*. London: Jessica Kingsley.

Stephens, Cassie. 2017. *Clay Lab for Kids: 52 Projects to Make, Model, and Mold with Air-Dry, Polymer, and Homemade Clay*. Beverly, MA: Quarry Books.

——. 2019. *Stitch and String Lab for Kids: 40+ Creative Projects to Sew, Embroider, Weave, Wrap, and Tie*. Beverly, MA: Quarry Books.

Taguchi, Hillevi Lenz. 2011. "Investigating Learning, Participation and Becoming in Early Childhood Practices with a Relational Materialist Approach." *Global Studies of Childhood* 1 (1): 36–50.

Taylor, Terry. 2014. *Clay Play! 24 Whimsical Projects*. Mineola, NY: Dover.

Texley, Juliana, and Ruth M. Ruud. 2018. *Teaching STEM Literacy: A Constructive Approach for Ages 3 to 8*. St. Paul, MN: Redleaf Press.

Topal, Cathy Weisman, and Lella Gandini. 1999. *Beautiful Stuff! Learning with Found Materials*. Worcester, MA: Davis.

VanDerwater, Amy Ludwig. 2018. *With My Hands: Poems about Making Things*. New York: Clarion Books.

Wagner, Tony. 2012. *Creating Innovators: The Making of Young People Who Will Change the World*. New York: Scribner.

Wardrip, Peter S., and Lisa Brahms. 2014. "Mobile MAKESHOP: Preliminary Findings from Two School Sites." http://fablearn.stanford.edu/2014/wp-content/uploads /fl2014_submission_49.pdf.

——. 2015. "Learning Practices of Making: Developing a Framework for Design." Proceedings of the 14th International Conference on Interaction Design and Children, 375–78.

Wilkinson, Karen, and Mike Petrich. 2014. *The Art of Tinkering: Meet 150+ Makers Working at the Intersection of Art, Science and Technology*. San Francisco: Weldon Owen.

Wohlwend, Karen. 2008. "Play as a Literacy of Possibilities: Expanding Meanings in Practices, Materials, and Spaces." *Language Arts* 86 (2): 127–36.

——. 2013. *Literacy Playshop: New Literacies, Popular Media, and Play in the Early Childhood Classroom*. New York: Teachers College Press.

Index